The
MILLION
DOLLAR
ORGANIZER®

365 Tips for Professional
Union Organizers

by

Bob Oedy

edited by

James Teddy

Disclaimer

Union organizing involves risk. Please be advised that this publication is designed to provide authoritative information on union organizing and communication techniques. This book is sold with the understanding that the author and publisher are not providing legal or other professional services. If expert or legal advice is required, please seek the services of a licensed and competent professional.

The views expressed in this book are those of the author only and do not represent the views of any organization. The information included herein is believed to be accurate. However, should you find any mistakes, please contact us so we can improve this text and consider corrections in future editions. This book should be used as a general guide only; it was created to complement other texts. We urge you to read all of the available material on these subjects. This manual contains information on union organizing that is current up to the printing date. Learn as much as you can about union organizing and tailor the information to your individual, organization or union's needs.

This book is designed to educate and entertain. The publisher and author are not responsible for any damage caused or alleged to be caused either directly or indirectly by the information contained herein. If you decide you cannot agree with this statement, please return the book to the publisher for a full refund.

Thank you.

To Leslie, Wendsday, Zero, Dylan, Nick, and Max – You Rock!

Acknowledgements

Thank you to my wife Leslie for her encouragement during the writing of this book. Thank you to James Teddy for a fine editing job. To my supporters, readers, and followers I wish to convey my deepest appreciation. In solidarity.

Table of Contents

Introduction

"Authors go where the pain is." – Ann Rice

I had a revelation…

How many union organizers are out there, like a proverbial ship lost at sea? A storm has arrived, waves are crashing over the bow, and the wind is howling sending chills through the decks. If they don't take corrective action fast the ship will capsize. Their careers will be smashed upon the rocks, their family's livelihoods severely impacted, and reputations destroyed.

In a way, this book is a response to an S.O.S. call received during the third watch. You can only ignore a plea for help so long… "Isn't anyone going to help?" The radio crackles, then silence. "You're not going to go about business as usual are you?" More silence. There's that feeling in your gut. You've got to do something. That inner voice says, "you'll never be able to live with yourself if you don't."

I awoke at 3am and started working on an outline. If no one else is going to write this book, then I'm going to write it, and nothing and nobody is going to stop me. I couldn't write this book ten years ago. I didn't have enough experience. There weren't enough wins under my belt. The inner voice would never have allowed it.

As soon as the pen hit the paper on this manuscript, there was an overwhelming feeling of relief. Someone would finally do something to assist the organizer out there struggling amongst the sea. As the magnitude of the challenge began to unfold however, those annoying self-doubts started to show themselves. What if it's too late? What dangers lie in the darkness? The decision had been made. There's a certain freedom in resolve. Full speed ahead!

The Million Dollar Organizer®

Your story may be similar to the stories of many union organizers the author has had the pleasure of working with over the years. It starts with someone asking you to participate, even if only as a volunteer. At some point you realize if you don't continue to be active, there may not be anyone else to take your place. This is indicative of many challenges the labor movement faces. There are few people with a real interest in the day-to-day operation of a union, especially recruiting new members. Once someone recognizes your interest in performing the work you are likely to be hired.

The next challenge is to stay employed. Most have some initial success as a union organizer, but the challenge is to stick around long enough to make a difference in the community you serve. Being a successful union organizer takes a commitment to lift-up vulnerable workers, show them there is dignity in work and give them hope. It's these ideals of justice and solidarity that makes our work as union organizers worth pursuing. You won't get rich doing this type of work, but it's important. If we stick around long enough, one day we'll look at our social security statement and realize we've been paid over a million dollars doing what we love.

What's Killing Our Unions?

We'll need to carefully maneuver the minefield of local union politics. Someone once described union hierarchy as a "snake pit." That's always stuck with me. Turnover rate of union organizers is the most important and least likely to be studied issue facing the labor movement. Few appear concerned with the fact that every month, experienced, well trained, professional union organizers are replaced with novices. Many organizers burn-out and leave on their own, some are terminated, and others are promoted to different positions. Other factors, that will increasingly affect unions as the baby boom generation ages, will be the number of professional union organizers retiring and dying. The good news for younger persons planning to make union organizing a career is, there should be plenty of employment opportunities in the coming years.

Where to Start

Most new organizers rely on bottom-up tactics because they can experience fast results with minimal training. It's not hard to recruit new members. It's a simple question of going out and talking to nonunion workers and convincing them to join. In fact, in many cases, the phone is already ringing with people who want to join. Callers have usually heard about the good wages and benefits, as well as free or low-cost training. When workers find themselves being taken advantage of, it's common for them to call the union to see what is available.

Union members can be the best source of referrals. To speed up recruiting while maintaining a high standard, ask members of your union to keep an eye out for qualified nonunion workers. They know if another worker is competent. Provide these volunteers with your business cards and any other wage and benefit information that is available. Most members will be happy to do this.

365 Tips for Professional Union Organizers

1. Commit to Union Organizing as a Career

"Don't judge each day by the harvest you reap, but by the seeds that you plant."
- Robert Louis Stevenson

Make the decision to advance your career from fledgling organizer to professional union organizer to Million Dollar Organizer®. Don't worry about having a fallback position. Too many novice organizers keep their tools at-the-ready in case things don't work out. Here's a better idea. Be determined to succeed no matter what. Are you familiar with the legend of Hernan Cortes? He was the Spanish Commander who ordered his troops to "burn the ships" to cut off chances of retreat. Like Cortes, go boldly in the direction of your dreams. Believe in yourself. Prove futurist, Alvin Toffler wrong. He predicted in 2007 that the job of Union Organizer will disappear within twenty years.

Shortly after being hired, a study concluded that the average union organizer position in my area lasted only 2 ½ years. My takeaway was, "then don't be average!"

Is Union Organizing for You?

Union organizing requires certain skills, long hours and time away from home. It can be exhausting work but it's also incredibly satisfying. Is it worth the sacrifice? Ask yourself these questions to find out………

1. Do you have good people skills?

Would you describe yourself as being a good listener, communicator or persuader? As an organizer, you will need to have these skills and more because you will be reaching out to workers and asking them to take a chance on a better future. These abilities are valued by organizations trying to gain influence and market share. It takes a certain type of individual to motivate people to embrace change.

2. Are you a self-starter?

For you to be an effective organizer you are going to have to get out in the field and contact the people doing the work. You can't wait to be told what to do. You must have a plan. That doesn't mean you shouldn't take orders or be team player, on the contrary. You just don't have the luxury of waiting around for things to happen by themselves.

3. Are you outgoing?

Approaching workers requires an organizer to put oneself out there. You have to be comfortable with yourself in order to make the contacts needed to be successful. This is not for the faint of heart. You're going to have to deal with a lot of rejection. You will need to be able to brush it off and not take it personal. Then come back again and again until the person is ready because you understand the value of organizing.

4. Are you an active member?

Although some unions hire outside the union most require that you are already a member because it's believed that a person will have a vested interest in the success of the organization. Being an active member means regularly attending meetings, activities and volunteering your time to help your union gain strength. Make an effort to volunteer on a picket line or on a precinct walk. Find some way to contribute your time and talents.

5. Are you already organizing?

Are you referring candidates? Are you helping workers? You may be surprised to hear it described as organizing, but that is what you are doing, recruiting people to consider a better more profitable way of working and conducting business.

Hopefully, these questions have shed some light on the subject of union organizing and helped you discover if union organizing is for you. The labor movement needs activists dedicated to increasing its membership and influence. If this describes you, consider union organizing for a career. It can be very challenging and rewarding.

2. Know Why We Organize

Top 5 Reasons for Organizing

Have you ever wondered, "Why do we organize?" It's a good question. Here are 5 reasons for union organizing and why you need to get involved today.

1. Increase Wages for Union Members – When a union controls the work in an area it is in a better position to negotiate higher wages for workers. Increased union market share ensures unions will be the predominant player in their industry and able to bargain from a point of strength. More members mean better contract negotiations. The leadership of your union knows this and that is why they are working to increase market share. It will help in future

contract negotiations. It's a fact that areas, where union density is the highest, tend to have higher rates of pay than those that don't. Union members earn 27% higher wages than nonunion workers according to the U.S. Dept. of Labor.

2. Increase Retirement and Health Benefits – The more people contributing into a retirement and health plan the stronger the plan will be. This is just one of the many reasons to actively recruit new members into the union. Fully 81% of union members have medical coverage while only 50% of nonunion workers have medical coverage, according to the U.S. Bureau of Labor Statistics. Similarly, union workers have pensions 72% of the time compared to only 15% of nonunion workers.

3. Improve Working Conditions - Unions give workers a voice in the workplace. This results in a safer working environment and a more democratic approach to solving problems on the job. The greater the strength of the union the more influence that workers have for improving conditions throughout the industry.

4. More Employment Opportunities – Encouraging union companies to bid work that might otherwise go nonunion helps employ members.

5. Fight Corporate Greed - Unions are under attack by well-funded nonunion corporate industry groups bent on turning back the clock on wage increases and worker rights (ie: Associated Builders and Contractors, Inc., Center for Union Facts, National Right to Work). Their attorneys actively lobby against workplace safety rules, prevailing wage laws and project labor agreements. They spend millions of dollars each year in attempts to stifle gains by labor through expensive litigation and support of politicians who oppose unions. The way to counter such attacks is by aggressively organizing the entire industry.

You can help your union organize by volunteering to:

1. Serve on a volunteer committee

2. Picket jobsites

3. House call nonunion workers

4. Voter registration

5. Phone banking

6. Precinct walking

7. Hand billing

8. Bannering

These are just a few of the ways you can help organize your industry. Get involved in the process and become a more active participant. Ask a union representative how you can help. You will find that you "get much more out of it than you ever put in", as they say. You can create change in the workplace and improve people's lives.

Unions are actively seeking additional members and employers to grow their ranks. Large numbers of union members are expected to retire while at the same time many young people are choosing to attend college or pursue other career paths.

The labor movement has been focusing money and resources toward organizing at an unprecedented level since the mid 1980's. This trend is expected to increase.

Commit to organizing your entire industry. Organizing is a vital mission and the responsibility of every union member. Stand up for justice and worker solidarity and never back down.

3. Start Your Own Union Organizing Library

"A mind that is stretched by new experience can never go back to its old dimensions." - Oliver Wendell Holmes

Successful people read books, magazines, newspapers. They scour libraries, websites, and lists for any possible nugget of information that might answer their question or offer a quicker solution. Here are 5 books for union organizers chosen by the author. Reading these will give you a broader sense of Labor's struggles while providing some needed tools to help you organize better. Perhaps this list will help reveal titles you have not yet read and encourage you to continue your search.

1. Win More Union Organizing Drives by Jason Mann

This book is a guidebook for field organizers. Jason Mann is well acquainted with the daily struggles organizers face when building relationships with workers. You can put many of the ideas to work immediately.

2. Great Labor Quotations; Sourcebook and Reader by Peter Bollen

Mr. Bollen put together a fine collection of quotes from Labor's greatest leaders. It's inspirational as well as readable. Reading quotes from long past labor activists helps to remind us that we are all fighting similar struggles. The names and the places have changed but things such as living wages, medical care and retiring with dignity are the same issues fought for today. This book is a joy to read and you can rely on it to give you a shot of inspiration when you need it.

3. Organize to Win; New Research on Union Strategies by Kate Bronfenbrenner

Organize to Win is on the syllabus for many organizing classes. There are case studies and actual campaigns that are highlighted by various organizers from different industries. It's interesting to see how different unions approach the subject of organizing. The author supports the use of data in the form of surveys, research, and analysis to gauge worker's attitudes during campaigns.

4. The Campaign Guide; Organizing the Construction Industry by the AFL-CIO Building and Construction Trades Department

This is a spiral reference guide designed to lie flat, that organizers can turn to for answers about legal questions that relate to organizing. For example, let's say you were wondering what the different types of picketing are and what constitutes a secondary boycott? You would simply refer to the chapter on Picketing in the Construction Industry and voila you have your answer. The sections on communicating with workers and forming alliances are very practical. This book is not available in stores.

5. Bigger Labor; A Crash Course for Construction Union Organizers by Bob Oedy

Whether you just got hired, or are a seasoned veteran, if you want to succeed in construction organizing, Bigger Labor will show you the way. You'll learn the nuts and bolts of construction organizing – the things they never taught you in the apprenticeship. Plus, this book is chock full of useful worksheets and checklists, so you can take what you learn and apply it immediately and directly to your organizing campaign.

4. Master the Organizer Evaluation

You've been assigned to attend an organizer evaluation, put on by your union to assess your ability as a union organizer. Regardless of your skill and experience, this is not going to be a walk-in-the-park.

Unions are implementing a tough new 25-point evaluation process to screen out unqualified applicants for union organizer positions. If you aren't ready to hit the ground running in a high stakes strategic organizing campaign you won't pass. How you perform here, could affect the rest of your organizing career.

Here are five things you must do to master the organizer evaluation.

1. Be prepared to write a strategic organizing plan.

One assignment requires writing a strategic plan for a fictitious company highlighted during the three-day event. The plan should include such things as; goals, timelines, benchmarks, issues, leaders, meetings, employee list, volunteer organizing committee, house calls, target date for filing, handbills, mailings, emails, itemized expenses, etc. It's expected to be completed and turned in the next morning.

2. Take detailed notes before, during and after each role play.

Yes, that's right. You're going to be doing role play. It's designed to get you out of your comfort zone to see if you can answer questions extemporaneously. Most organizers excel at this, so have fun!

Each role play is related to the same campaign. In other words, whether you are communicating with a worker or addressing a volunteer organizing committee its likely part of the same campaign. The information will later be needed when writing your strategic organizing plan. It's important to remember for example leader's names, how many employees a company has, etc. Take notes throughout the process to refer to later.

3. Look sharp! Dress business casual.

You won't get a second chance to make a good first impression, so dress nice. Guys; wear a sports coat, ladies; dress conservatively. Shorts, flip-flops, hats or old jeans are not appropriate for an event of this type.

4. Listen for clues and urge the person to act.

Some participants have expressed disappointment with their assessment score in one category; Ability to Motivate Others to Act. For whatever reason, they didn't feel they received adequate credit for doing so during role play. Compensate for this by giving each person a specific call to action and asking for a commitment.

5. Get plenty of rest.

There's a tendency for people to want to blow off some steam after a long day in a classroom, especially when traveling far from family and friends. Be careful not to stay out too late or drink in excess. Get plenty of rest. Eat healthy and be ready for the challenges ahead.

By following these five simple tips you will master the organizer evaluation. You will receive the highest possible score because you will be on top of your game, look sharp, be better informed and avoid common mistakes others have made.

Good Luck!

5. Join Toastmasters International

Communication is the key to successful union organizing. Members of Toastmaster's International practice public speaking, leadership, and active listening in a fun and supportive environment. They also plan and conduct meetings, speech contests, seminars, and conferences. Consider joining Toastmasters International to elevate your own communication skills and network with like-minded individuals dedicated to self-improvement.

Toastmasters was started to help individuals practice public speaking skills. It's grown worldwide and helped millions of people. You can find specialized clubs of all kinds including several in the labor movement. Every local union should encourage their members to join Toastmasters. It's a great way to prepare future leaders.

After attending just one meeting, I noticed speakers using "filler-words" in speeches. People rely on certain crutch words such as "so, uh, um, like, you know," and others without being aware. It can become a bad habit that negatively affects their ability to communicate. Later that week at an organizing conference I noted how often certain speakers used the same filler word. One well-known speaker used, "uh" over one hundred and fifty times in a five-minute presentation. Perhaps if it were a fifteen-minute presentation it might not have been so obvious. Other speakers didn't make that mistake. At the end of the conference, I rated the speakers for my own edification. The speaker who used the filler words appeared less prepared, less self-confident. The others were more interesting and seemed more comfortable in their own skin. It convinced me to become a member of Toastmasters if for no other reason than to fix my own shortcomings when it came to communication. Membership brought many opportunities to volunteer and serve. My goal was to earn Distinguished Toastmaster status, but in doing so I made some wonderful friends. They elected me club president, convinced me to compete in speech contests. Four years later, I won Division Governor of the Year and finally became a Distinguished Toastmaster.

Joining Toastmasters International was a great experience, one I recommend to anyone interested in improving their communication skills.

6. Know Your Numbers

How many elections did you win? What was the vote count? How many members were brought in? What was the percentage of representation cards signed? Financial leaders on television are always rattling-off numbers. They know exactly what's going on because they make a study of it. Business measures success by profit. Companies don't wait until the end of the year to take a measurement and neither should unions. Shareholders demand information quarterly. Three months is usually enough time to know if you're headed toward success or into the weeds. Adopt the mentality that business shares. Change course when needed. Be prepared to report the numbers to members and your supervisor when asked.

7. Connect via Social Media

"Happiness is something that comes into our lives through doors we don't even remember leaving open." - Rose Lane

Workers are online searching for jobs and services. Don't be invisible. Even the most stubborn holdouts eventually realize they need to connect via social media. Connect with people whatever way makes them feel most comfortable. Be sure to add a photo to your profile. People want to be able to connect a face with the name. It's always nice to be recognized.

While we're at it; let's connect. I'm on a variety of social networks

- Facebook.com/unionorganizer

- Facebook.com/boboedyauthor

- Twitter.com/unionorganizer

- Instagram.com/unionorganizer

- Linkedin.com/in/unionorganizer

Please consider reviewing my book online. Reviews sell books. Thanks!

8. Ask for Advice

Other union organizers have walked the path you're on. Ask for advice. It can save the union money and you a lot of time and effort. Sometimes we hesitate to ask peers for advice because we are concerned about appearing less competent. Another concern might be that the person will direct all your actions. The opposite is more likely. People are flattered when asked to share their expertise. Often, they'll give you options and steer you toward resources you wouldn't have found on your own. Remember, you're not under any obligation to take their advice if it sounds like it won't work.

9. Make a Great First Impression

Making a great first impression is so important, and it only takes a little more effort than a "good" first impression. It requires the same exact time, one to fifteen seconds depending whose research you believe. Smile more, be excited. Show more enthusiasm. Stand up straight and throw your shoulders back. No more wet noodle handshakes. No bone-crusher handshakes either. Give people your full, undivided attention. Look them right in the eyes. Have your business cards with you at the ready.

Today is a good time to buy that fancy business card holder you've always wanted. It will protect your cards from bending and getting dirty. You might be surprised how many people forget to carry their cards. What's the point of having a business card if it's left back at the office?

10. Return Every Call

It's easy to get distracted as an organizer. Every day brings more fires to put out so to speak. We get pushed and pulled in different directions and this creates the possibility for a candidate to fall through the cracks. Are you doing enough to follow up with candidates?

My guess is that there are opportunities for greater communication.

Take This Simple 3-Question Organizing Quiz to Discover How Good Your Follow Up Is

1) Do you return all your calls?

People expect to be contacted in a short period of time. If you don't, before long you get a bad reputation. By not returning calls you are sending a message that says, "you really aren't that important to me." This may not be the case, but there's an assumption. Imagine the opportunities you could be missing out on. Return every call and you will gain the respect of your candidates and coworkers.

2) Do you mail out follow up letters?

People will forget most of what you said on the phone. They will get lost on the way to your office. Some won't bring the documentation you require. Others will feel confused or neglected, not sure what you expected them to do next. Here's an opportunity to set the record straight by highlighting what was said in your telephone conversation. Provide a checklist of needed paperwork, an explanation of how you intend to help the person. You might even provide a map to your location with office hours and major cross streets. This will help to reinforce your instructions.

3) Do you gather enough information?

So, you have the persons first and last name, but do you have their address, phone number, and email address? How about knowing what companies the person has worked for, their level of education and certifications earned? Think how much better you will be able to serve the person if you had more ways to keep in touch. Give yourself plenty of options for contacting the person and give them options for contacting you.

There are some great reasons for doing this. For example; when things get busy you will rely on your database to fill positions or seek referrals of friends and coworkers. If a question comes up about a certain employer, you will know just who to contact to get the answer. You will have a better understanding of who the players in your industry are and better communication with those affected.

If you found yourself not taking advantage of follow up opportunities in my quiz, you're not alone. If you want the benefit of more members, improved satisfaction and, a higher percentage of retention then you need to act today.

11. Use Direct Mail

You've made initial contact with a potential candidate for your union, but he or she won't always follow through as you want them to. So, you need a fool-proof system to stay in touch until the candidate signs up. One way to do this is a series of direct mailings. It may seem like overkill at first, following up a phone call or a jobsite visit with letters via mail, but it's not. By initiating a system of regular follow-ups, you will stay in better touch with potential candidates and increase the number of workers who follow through, ultimately becoming members.

It may take five or six outreach efforts before you gain someone's trust. That's why regular follow-up is so important. "Average organizers" don't do this. Here's your chance to break out of the pack. Each time you reconnect with a potential candidate, you are reinforcing the message that you are credible and have something to offer. Do everything you can to convey the message that you are interested in helping every worker. You can accomplish this with a series of follow-up mailings.

These mailings should include specific instructions on what the next step is. The first letter gives a broad overview of the benefits of joining the union. Each consecutive letter elaborates on one key benefit. Try to make each letter different from the previous one in content and format. The first mailing might be on letterhead, the second could be a postcard, the third could be a brochure from your training facility, the fourth a newspaper article with a note attached and so on.

Mailer #1 is an initial letter sent to potential candidates who inquire about the union. Although on the phone or in person you may cover in detail exactly what is needed for membership, it helps to follow up via direct mail in case there was some confusion. If the person forgets what the next step in the process is the letter will act as a reminder. You can customize the letter to fit your needs or your union's requirements for membership. Consider putting this on business stationary with your letterhead on top and mailing it in a #10 envelope.

Mailer #2 is a postcard that reads, "Wish you were here." This mailing will elaborate on the benefit "better pay." On the back, put information about how by not contacting you by the deadline the candidate missed out on earnings.

Mailer #3 is a brochure from the training facility, if available. Place this mailer in an 8X10 manila envelope. Attach your business card with a letter that elaborates the benefits of high-quality training.

Mailer #4 is a copy of a recent newspaper article on the importance of medical and dental coverage. Consider downloading the article from the internet and use a good quality copy so that it will be easily read. Attach a note with your business card.

Mailer #5 is a pen or pencil with the name of the vision care provider stuffed in a bubble envelope, your business card, and a letter. People tend to open lumpy mail. Here you will briefly elaborate on the benefits of having vision care coverage.

Mailer #6 is a leaflet with a photo of a member and his family. Below is a testimonial about the cost savings of having paid prescription coverage.

Mailer #7 is a comic strip about retirement with a note attached articulating the benefits of having a plan in place. Help the candidate visualize the union as the right organization to assist in achieving financial success.

To recap, with a fool-proof system for direct mail, you will be better connected with your candidates and have a greater response rate, which will likely result in more workers becoming union members. Customize each mailer to fit your individual situation. Send out a different mailer per candidate each week and try not to get discouraged if you don't get a response right away. Persistence is the key to good follow up, and it may take several communications before you build up the trust needed for a positive response.

12. Avoid Using Acronyms

We can get carried away with use of abbreviations for everything from the name of our union to job classifications and National Labor Relations Board. The problem is, not everyone is familiar with these acronyms and they can cause a lot of confusion. If you are speaking with other organizers familiar with these abbreviations it's one thing, but when speaking with members and workers make sure to explain everything and avoid using acronyms. It's good practice to simplify what we are saying so everyone can digest the information.

Several union organizers get together for regular monthly meetings. The turn-over rate being what it is, there may be a brand-new organizer every month or at least every other month. We, organizers, need to be aware of how acronyms can be confusing to people who are hearing them for the first time. Otherwise, we might file a ULP for a CW at the NLRB when all we needed was her DL so she could get FMLA. See what I mean?

13. Teach to Learn

For a subject to be taught properly it requires a full understanding of the details. Once you've become confident in your ability to demonstrate a given subject, that's when you realize you know the subject. Look for opportunities to mentor union members interested in organizing. Become a trainer. Break each task down to its simplest form. Ask yourself, "How could I demonstrate what I'm doing to someone who has never done this?" The answers will direct you on where to start and what steps to include.

When my first book, Bigger Labor; a crash course for construction union organizers was published I got invited to speak at an organizing conference. They agreed to buy copies in exchange for an hour-long training session. "Sure," I said. They weren't specific about the topic so I chose what would likely be the most interesting to the group.

Soon they called back asking if I could extend the training portion to 4 hours. Again, I agreed. They called back asking me to extend the four-hour session to eight hours. "Sure, why not," I said. Now I was in a pickle. I began to panic. Was there enough information in the book to cover eight full hours of training?

I began from page one, reviewing everything in the book. It would require graphics, a PowerPoint presentation, and handouts. There were teaching techniques that helped me learn what I wanted to include in my presentation. I drew on my own experiences sitting through training demonstrations and courses over the years to craft the perfect presentation. There would be breakout sessions and contests with prizes to keep the audience's attention. I relied on techniques and feedback from friends. These involved moving around the room to keep people's attention and asking open-ended questions to get people engaged. When the day came to put on the training, it went quite smooth. The audience loved it and I got some suggestions for future presentations. It was a learning experience for me as well as the audience.

Show Coworkers by Doing

A coworker trained me to access nonunion construction sites and speak to workers. He had mastered the technique. We visited a mixed-use project in Pasadena, but didn't see any workers. I was inclined to give up since we checked just about everywhere. He was undeterred however. I followed him down a dark corridor in the basement past boxes of materials, over loose cords and through puddles of water. He stopped at a door and appeared to listen signaling me to be quiet. He pushed the door open and walked in confidently. I was close behind. The entire crew, including supervision were having lunch warmed by the heat from the transformers. I was sure we were about to be run-off the job. He said loudly, "I knew we'd find you down here." You could hear a pin drop. "Listen very carefully," he said in a commanding voice. "We are looking for ten electricians like yourselves for a prevailing wage project in Glendale that starts Monday." The workers listened intently. Some were nodding in support as they looked at each other as if we just announced a raise. He motioned for me to hand out business cards and wage flyers. Everyone took a copy. "We've been keeping an eye on this project. You are doing a great job. When is this project scheduled to be occupied?" he asked. Someone mumbled a date. The General Foreman interrupted saying, "I can't believe you guys found us down here." We both laughed and hung around another minute or two before heading to the next job.

14. Send a Holiday Card

The most important habit in organizing is to follow up with people. The holidays are a great time to contact workers. Stay in touch over time to help build trust and familiarity.

It was a miserably hot August afternoon. The job was a student housing project at UCLA some 20 miles from the office. As I trudged up a flight of stairs I spotted a non-union electrician standing on a ladder terminating wires. I handed him a business card and moved on. He took the card and looked at it. I was halfway down the hallway when he shouted, "Hey! You're Bob Oedy!" "I've got your Christmas card on my fridge." I walked back to shake his hand. He told me he taped the Christmas card on his refrigerator as a reminder to call me. We talked for a few minutes. He has a son the same age as mine. Eventually, I got him to join.

The previous year a friend helped superimpose Happy Holidays with a Christmas theme on a photo of my son and I camping. People seemed to like it. Every person who called me that year received two mailings; a follow-up letter and a holiday card. The trick in making an impression with holiday cards is to either be the engine or the caboose. That year the cards were in the mail the day after Thanksgiving. In addition to dozens of calls, I received a ton of Holiday cards in return. You can use a handwriting font to make your mailing labels look more personal. The most important thing is to get them mailed. You'll be amazed at the results.

15. Be Prepared

Have your organizing materials, leaflets, handbills, business cards, sign-in sheets, contact card, etc. printed and ready to go. Before you visit a workplace, you need to have a plan. Ask yourself, "What's my purpose for visiting this particular project?" Are you trying to identify which contractors are performing work in your area? Are you trying to recruit new members into your union? Perhaps you want to identify Occupational Safety and Health

Administration (OSHA) safety violations. Whatever the reason, make sure you have a plan.

Different situations call for different tactics, there is no right or wrong way to approach workers. It just comes down to using your own personal style. Are you going to be with a group of organizers or by yourself? Will the employees be taking their lunch break? All these situations come into play and will help to determine what strategy you use.

Some organizers are aggressive and tend to be high profile so that the employer, as well as the workers, know that they are onsite to recruit for the union. In this case, they might dress like a supervisor or a "white hat." It takes a direct delivery, and it results in engaging the employee about working conditions and pay right from the start. Many organizers use this approach, and it works well for them. They tend to get people talking and in doing so gather a lot of valuable information about an employer and the employees.

You may prefer a more-subtle approach engaging workers when they are alone or in small groups. In these situations, you may be less aggressive in choosing to plant a seed of interest by offering your business card or leaflet saying, "Hey, when you get a chance, look at this flyer. If you are interested give me a call at this number." I find this approach leads to additional questions and is likely to lead to productive dialogue.

If you are on a construction site, for example, wear a hardhat and work boots regardless of whether the workers are wearing theirs. Bring plenty of business cards and leaflets to distribute to workers. Bring a clipboard, paper, and pen so you can write down workers' names and record your observations. If additional personal protective equipment is required, such as safety glasses, goggles, vest, or earplugs, don't wait to be told you need them. Be proactive. This serves four purposes: you set an example of professionalism, you blend into the worksite, you eliminate an excuse for the contractor to "run you off," and it protects you from safety hazards.

Carry a copy of your union's workers' compensation policy. Eventually, you'll run into a contractor who claims you're not allowed on the project because it doesn't want the liability if you get hurt. Carry a copy of any letter your attorney provides requesting access to jobsites. Bring an OSHA Complaint Form so you can fill it out on site if you see a violation. This makes a great conversation starter if you accessed the job and are then asked to leave. Bring a Project Information Form so you can fill it out on site minimizing your chance of forgetting to record key information. The key is to always be prepared when reaching out to workers.

16. Identify Contractors

9 Ways to Identify Contractors Before Stepping Foot on a Project

You've been assigned to check on a project in your jurisdiction. The address doesn't ring a bell. Is it a union job or not? Is the contractor hostile toward the union? To make a proper assessment you'll need to gather information.

Here are 9 ways to identify contractors before stepping foot on a project.

1. Visit your city's planning department

2. Search the address on the internet

3. Check the internet for bid results

4. Attend bid openings

5. Call the awarding agency or customer

6. Check the gate for signs

7. Look for banners on fences and trailers

8. Scan parking areas for marked trucks and trailers

9. Scan gang boxes for company names

Know who you are dealing with and you'll be better prepared. Good luck!

17. Research Past Campaigns

When a campaign fails there are tell-tale signs as to why. Review all the information available. Some organizations require a report or brief after a campaign. It's a good practice. A campaign summary should include such things as issues, dates, timeline, percentage of cards, tally of votes, things learned, etc. Such information will be invaluable to yourself and others in future campaigns or if you decide to revive a campaign later. It's an opportunity to review strengths and weaknesses before committing resources. Request a copy of the campaign summary or look it up on your organizations reporting platform.

Reviewing a campaign summary is a great way to leverage everything learned for greater results on future campaigns. A campaign summary can also be utilized to prepare for similar campaigns.

18. Ask Members for Leads

Union members can be the best source for referrals. They often know others who are not yet represented and are interested. These leads can be among the most productive. To speed up recruiting while maintaining a high standard, ask members of your union to keep an eye out for qualified nonunion workers. They know if another worker is competent. Provide these volunteers with your business cards and any other wage and benefit information that is available. Most members will be more than happy to do this.

19. Network with Peers

No one succeeds by themselves. Make time to connect with union organizers, both from your union and others. Exchange contact information and stay in touch. Solidarity is needed more now than ever before. We all have a lot to offer and the labor movement needs our combined energies if it's to survive. Refer interested candidates to respective locals. Ask to be notified when employment opportunities arise. Always keep your options for advancement open.

20. Network with Community Leaders

Whether union organizers are in a small town or a big city, connecting with community leaders can be advantageous. We want to be in touch with the movers and shakers. We want to know who decision makers are, and perhaps more importantly, we want them to know who we are. There will be opportunities to work together for a common good. There will undoubtedly be some issues where we will find ourselves on opposing sides. By networking with community leaders, we can affect needed change in support of union members.

21. Practice Active Listening

Worker's will tell us everything we need to know if we ask the right questions and give them our full attention. One of the keys to success as a union organizer is to be a good listener. This skill is tough for some people because we're passionate about being a union member and can't wait to talk about all the benefits of membership. The medical benefits are fantastic! What do you mean the employer doesn't offer medical coverage? Don't you know they're ripping you off? Our pension plans will allow you to retire with dignity! What are you going to do for retirement? Why, I know this one retiree that's been pulling his pension for twenty years! Can you believe that? Twenty years! And… STOP!!!!

We must force ourselves to stop. It's the most difficult thing to do, but we must to do our job correctly. Sure, we can't wait to tell everyone about the benefits of being in a union, but let's face it, not everyone is interested in being in a union. An organizer who spends a little more time listening will be doing the candidate a real service.

Shortly after being hired as a union organizer, a young man contacted me. He had heard that he could earn substantially more than he was earning at the time. I assured him it was true and immediately started to tell him about all the benefits of being accepted into the apprenticeship program. We were going to give him a job with a decent hourly wage, invest thousands in his education, send him to school for training. When he completed the five-year program, he was going to be a journeyman earning a substantial wage. I completed his paperwork and sent him down to be interviewed and placed into the program. The next day, he arrived for his interview, and the first questions he was asked was, "So you want to be an electrician?" He answers, "Well not really, see I'm trying to earn enough money so my brother and I can open a muffler shop."

Ouch! See, he probably tried to tell me that, but I was too busy flapping my jaw, telling him all about the benefits and rewards of being in the union. If I could have just forced myself to listen a little more, I could have avoided the embarrassment that followed when my boss called with an unbelievable story about the candidate that wanted to open a muffler shop. It didn't stop there, either. A meeting followed, and a checklist was created with a list of topics to discuss with every candidate before he or she was sent to be placed in the program. I can laugh about it now, but it was embarrassing at the time.

Another time while meeting with a potential union employer at his office, I spotted an unusual stuffed fish hanging on the wall. Curious, I asked, "Did you catch that fish?" He smiled and said, "Let me tell you about that fish." A half-hour later, I knew more about his company then I ever could have by doing research or speaking with the employees. I just asked a simple question and then allowed him the courtesy of my full attention without any interruptions.

22. Don't Assume You Know the Issue

"Real knowledge is to know the extent of one's ignorance." - Confucius

Keep an open mind when confronted with worker's issues. Avoid making judgements before having all the facts. We may have had similar experiences in the past, however, each situation is different. Ask questions to clarify details. Gather as much information together to get a true picture of circumstances. There are many factors that can cause miscommunication. Some words have multiple meanings. There are nonverbal cues, bias, family issues, language, culture, environment, illness, and interpretation which play a role. For these reasons we should not assume we know an issue before hearing all sides.

23. Know Your State's Labor Laws

Laws vary by jurisdiction. Know your state's labor laws and familiarize yourself with the departments responsible for overseeing compliance. You can find information online on their website. In the state of California for example, it's the Department of Industrial Relations www.dir.ca.gov . The United States Department of Labor has a comprehensive list at https://www.dol.gov/whd/contacts/state_of.htm .

24. Avoid Making Promises

Let management be the one making empty promises. Their reputation is already tainted. Once they realize the workers are organizing, talk of wage increases, bonuses and promotions begin. If you inoculate the workers in advance, they'll recognize management's promises as just another trick. A year later, whether you win or lose the campaign the workers will know the union kept their word and the company didn't.

What could be more important than authenticity? What trait could do more harm to a campaign than lack of integrity? Therefore, we don't make promises. Successful union organizers let management climb out-on-a-limb. See them out there with no place to go but down. We allow it to happen and eventually, the workers recognize the union is on their side.

A young woman named Anna attended a meeting to discuss organizing the call center where she worked. According to Anna, the previous year during her job interview, she was told by the employer significant pay increases would be coming soon, work conditions were relaxed and the crew were like family. She was sent to an anti-union meeting her first day on the job. The employer told her, "Some of the workers here want a union and they don't like you because you're a new-hire so stay away from them." She did as she was told. A year later, however, it became painfully clear that everything promised to her in the job interview was a lie. There were no pay increases coming. She found this out talking with coworkers who had been there for years. Work conditions were intolerable. They timed her going to the restroom. One day the restroom on her floor was being cleaned, so she went downstairs and found a long line for the women's room. Fearing reprisal, she ran back upstairs without using the facilities and went back to work. Anna was so passionate, she cried relating her story. We knew she would be the perfect leader for the campaign. Anna was a hard-working, dedicated employee with integrity. The union was there to help her and her coworkers, but we made no promises.

25. Give People Three Solutions

Have you noticed it's easier to motivate people when you give options? It puts the person in charge. They make the decision that works best for them. Sometimes you can steer a person in the right direction by giving two not so desirable options and one which is the obvious choice. Some organizers treat candidates like there is only one solution to their problems – go union. There are many possible solutions. Going union might be the best, but share some other possibilities and let the individual decide.

Sometimes when given a lead, I'll follow up only to find the person is unhappy with the current employer and wants to work for a union shop. I like to give the person three solutions to their problem. The first might be to organize the current employer and get a union contract. The second might be to be placed in the apprenticeship and work for a union contractor. The third might be to rally some co-workers together and march into the boss's office demanding a raise. Any of these options could work. Offering a person, a choice of solutions gives an individual a better understanding of the commitment required to succeed.

As a single dad, I always enjoyed taking my son places on weekends. He was content staying home and playing video games. When given the option he'd pick video games almost every time. All those hours spent in front of a screen can cause kids problems. Instead, I began offering three options. We could go to the beach and fly kites. We could go for a hike in the local mountains, or we could stay home and do yard work together. Most of the time he picked going to the beach to fly kites. Those were some great times! He convinced me to take him to an arcade afterward most days, but it was part of the compromise. He'll make a great negotiator someday.

26. Ask for Employee List

An employee list is the cornerstone of every successful organizing campaign. Ask for it, up front. If the person can produce an employee list quickly it's a good sign. The best employee lists include every person involved in the company. These are usually only available to key personnel, someone on the inside. The importance of an accurate list cannot be overstated. In absence of a company created list, you can have the workers write down everyone they know to be working for the company.

One of my favorite organizing campaigns involved field technicians spread over a large geographical area. Workers were provided utility trucks, but because their area was so spread out they almost never saw their coworkers. At an initial meeting to assess whether the group would be a good target for organizing one of the workers who worked in the office produced an employee list. The list was disguised as a bowling league. He had an electronic version that was encrypted so only key people within the campaign were able to access the information.

During the last weeks of the campaign management resorted to holding their meetings in an SUV parked in the company parking lot because they were convinced the office was bugged. They didn't realize one of the managers was sympathetic to the plight of the hourly workers and was feeding us information. That's how we knew their every move.

In my book, Bigger Labor, there's a story about a candidate who shared that he was just released from prison. He said he had prior experience, but because he couldn't prove it at the time, wasn't able to come into membership at the desired rate. He asked me to recommend a nonunion shop where he could apply in the meantime. He was on parole and needed to find work quickly. I provided a list of local contractors that were hiring and asked that if he were hired, to please try and stay in touch because I would like information about the employees for a future organizing campaign. He was hired right away and made a foreman. Later that week, he faxed me a list of every employee in the company and their telephone numbers. I called every one of the workers and not one was satisfied with the level of pay they were receiving. He was successful at convincing two of the workers from his jobsite to contact us and join our ranks, and those workers are still members today.

27. Ask for Organizational Chart

An organizational chart or "org chart" for short, gives a view of the internal structure of the company by title or department. You need to understand the corporate hierarchy to effectively organize the workers. An org chart will tell you the pecking order, who is a supervisor and who is being supervised. It's important to know when determining the size of the unit. Many large corporations publish their org charts on their website. Small companies might not have one. In this case, you can ask a trusted worker to create one from the knowledge the individual has gained working with the employer. When you ask for an employee list, ask for an org chart.

An organizer was approached by a group of employees of a municipal water district in southern California. They were interested in being represented by a union. When asked how many employees worked for the water district the organizer was told there were 94. The employee list the workers provided seemed to prove this point. However, while researching the org chart on the water district website the organizer discovered two other groups under the same department. Each of the units had about the same number of workers. Suddenly the number of cards needed was triple the original estimate. When informed by the organizer, the workers were surprised but it was clear from studying the org chart. The campaign would take longer than expected, but at least they went forward knowing the size of the group instead of being blindsided after the petition was filed. You can learn the size and scope of the operation by studying the org chart, so ask for it.

28. Ask Leaders to Rate Coworker Support

Once we've identified who the obvious leaders are to help organize a group, ask them to rate coworker support for organizing a union at their workplace. Each workers name on the employee list is considered using a 1 – 5 Scale of likely support. 1 being low support and 5 being high support. This will give an idea where the campaign stands, and help direct where to focus energy and resources.

29. Simplify the Process

Simplify processes to increase our effectiveness. Is there an obstacle to progress for the union? Take the time to examine how tasks are completed. What's not working? How could we increase our effectiveness? What could save money and or time? Implement changes to increase competitiveness.

Anyone who's purchased real estate has seen this in progress. A real estate professional will gather client's information early so when clients finally decide to purchase they already have the paperwork completed. All that is needed is a signature and the date.

Somewhere along the line, someone must have noticed if the customer had to sit while the paperwork was completed things didn't go so smooth. As a result, almost the entire industry has adopted the simplified process of having paperwork completed in advance and only needing a signature and date to complete the transaction. Could we implement a similar process? What process could we simplify to increase our effectiveness or that of the industry?

Over the years, I've seen local unions adopt changes such as online dues payments that have saved countless dollars and freed up resources for organizing. We might be limited to what we can do as organizers, but we can certainly make recommendations to the people in charge.

30. Check Website for List of Customers

Companies tend to add names of other companies they do business with as well as projects they've worked on to promote themselves. You can find out about these relationships on the company website.

31. Acquaint Yourself with the D.O.L. Website

The United States Department of Labor (DOL) is the federal agency responsible for protecting workers, job-applicants, and retirees. – Website: https://www.dol.gov The D.O.L. is a behemoth covering a myriad of topics of concerns for workers including wage theft, work visa's, disability, veterans' employment, workplace safety, employee compensation, fiduciary responsibilities, and more. By acquainting yourself with the D.O.L. website you'll be able to better serve workers in distress.

32. Attend Apprenticeship Graduations

Keep in touch with apprentice candidates through the process which may take years to accomplish. Be there as they struggle. Celebrate their victories. Some apprenticeships host a graduation dinner. This can be a formal event with family and friends in attendance as well as politicians and industry leaders. Awards are sometimes given out for such things as Apprentice of the Year or Perfect Attendance.

At one such event, bored-to-death and needing to stretch my legs, a candidate stopped me on the way to the restroom. He leaped from his seat at the opposite side of a table. We immediately recognized each other. Years earlier, we spent a great deal of time gathering the necessary documents to get him in. He was from the Philippines and all his paperwork, diplomas and transcripts had to be translated to English. Shaking my hand vigorously he said something to his family in Tagalog. They all got up and introduced themselves. His beautiful wife in broken English and with tears in her eyes thanked me for helping her husband get in the program. She was holding my hand with both hers as she introduced their two kids and her mom and dad. The importance of the job we do as union organizers was cemented at that moment. Forget the individual if you will. We are affecting entire families. We are lifting people from poverty. Up until that moment, apprenticeship graduations were just another in a long line of duties as someone on staff. My girlfriend at the time had no interest in attending an apprenticeship graduation. She had endured enough work-related outings. Exhausted after a long week of work it was the last thing on my list of fun things to do. Still, it was important. Someone had to be there. It's important to celebrate milestones. If for no other reason but to remind ourselves why we organize.

Encourage apprentices to attend their own graduation ceremonies. During that final year of an apprenticeship, it's easy to get bored or overwhelmed. You just want the experience to be over. Toward the end of my own apprenticeship, working as an inside wireman electrician in Los Angeles, spending another evening with my classmates was the last thing on my mind.

The invitation arrived in the mail. It was quickly round-filed. Thankfully, a female friend inquired about the ceremony. It was to be held in the Main Ballroom of the Queen Mary in Long Beach,

California. She told me the story of how her soon-to-be husband skipped his own apprenticeship graduation the previous year. There she was all-dressed-up the night of the big event. Her fiancé changed his mind and decided against going. There was no way she was allowing me to skip my graduation. We were going. She was going to be my date. The invitation got pulled out of the trash and the RSVP was made.

The graduation dinner was a black-tie affair. No expenses were spared. My date was stunning. We had a blast! Seeing my classmates, who normally wore dirty jeans and tee shirts, all dressed up was a trip. Up until that point, we were treated like kids. My first day on the job, a journeyman referred to us apprentices as, "scum sucking whale shit." One evening during a storm, with the road washed out and people being plucked off the roofs of their cars in the Sepulveda Basin making it to class seemed impossible. The school made it clear though if we didn't make it to the class that night we would be marked absent. No excuses. Somehow through sheer determination that didn't happen. Now the leadership of the local union as well as the training trust were honoring us as graduates or Journeymen. It felt damn good! Each of us was called by name and received cheers by our classmates and instructors. We all received a graduation certificate, union medallion and custom hard-hat. Later, those of us with perfect attendance received a plaque, tool bag with union logo and had our picture taken for the newsletter. It was an unforgettable night.

33. Check Sample Ballot for Accuracy

After filing an RC Petition with the National Labor Relations Board and receiving a copy of the sample election ballot, check it for accuracy. Board agents are people too. They get overwhelmed and make errors like everyone else. Make sure all information is included and everything is spelled correctly. If anything is unclear or you have concerns about the ballot, alert the board agent right away. The election ballot should have language on it that asserts the boards neutrality in the process.

Instruct supporters to simply mark the box of their choice with an "X". Remind them not to sign the ballot or make any identifiable markings as this may void the ballot. If they make an error, they can ask the board agent for a new one.

34. Ask for Forgiveness Not Permission

In organizing, it's much better to beg forgiveness than ask permission. If you really want to make a difference, you're going to have to take some risks. You are going to have to put yourself out there and see what happens. Be proactive. Meet challenges head-on. Of course, you're going to have good days and bad days, but to be an exceptional organizer, you're going to need to practice the fundamentals of being a self-starter and having goals. You must decide that you're going to be the one to make a difference. Organizers are problem solvers; they're self-motivated. It's not the type of job in which you wait for an assignment, and then do the work. If you wait for someone to tell you what to do, you'll be waiting for a long time.

An organizing conference was attended by organizers from various states who gathered to create a strategic plan. A consultant was brought in to moderate the event. Ideas were tossed around, and substantive conversations resulted. An outline was written up with each organizer assigned a responsibility. No idea was too small or too large, and everyone was encouraged to air their concerns. Things started to look like we were finally going to tackle this behemoth. We were finally casting aside our differences and focusing on the problem at hand. That's when someone made the following recommendations; "Let's not do anything for 30 days and see what happens."

You might think such a statement was met with laughter, but it wasn't. If it was said as a joke, we would have laughed, but it wasn't a joke and this person had significant clout. My disappointment must have been obvious. A colleague leaned over and whispered, "If the other side could see us right now, they'd all breathe a little easier."

In many ways, this is systemic of the problem labor unions face today. Some people don't understand the implications of waiting around to see what happens. Consistent and persistent efforts must be made across the board. As early as 2008, I warned that labor was at a tipping point (Bigger Labor, Union Organizer Press). We're way past that point now. Consider this all the permission you need.

35. Avoid Responding to Every Accusation

In an NLRB election, the employer will use many arguments to persuade workers to vote against union representation. Many of these claims will be greatly exaggerated or complete falsehoods altogether. They will purposely inflate the required dues workers are expected to pay or argue employees will no longer have the right to communicate directly with management. Your natural reaction will be to respond to these accusations by the employer with a well-written rebuttal. There will be times when you should clarify the union's position to explain the process to the workers. In most cases, however, to do so will give the employer a distinct advantage. Now the employer is controlling the dialogue or direction of the campaign. This is a consequence seen too often in unsuccessful organizing efforts. The employer hurls an accusation, the union responds. The employer concocts the worst possible scenario; the union responds again. Soon the union's message of respect, fairness, and dignity gets mired in the minutia of payroll deductions, administration costs and internal processes.

Once off into the weeds it's difficult but not impossible to refocus campaign messaging. There was a campaign I was brought in along with some others to help in the final week before the election. The organizers had done a great job maintaining interest and being visible but somehow gotten off course and allowed the employer to control the messaging.

The organizers were exhausted working long hours away from home and it showed on their faces. When we met for a debrief the campaign was described as a "battle." They made it sound as if we were somehow in danger. They had stayed up late nights fashioning daily leaflets in response to canned innuendos leveled by the employer. Everyone was running in circles. They weren't eating well, weren't exercising, and missed their families back home. With just one week to go before the vote, no one was going anywhere, however. Over the next few days, with the help of additional staff, the group managed to get the union's message back on track. No more late nights transcribing two-page leaflets explaining union policies. The new focus allowed the VOC members to do one-on-one worker outreach with holdouts. We were no longer responding to accusations and instead cementing support for a win.

36. Save All Correspondence

We can keep ourselves out of a lot of trouble by saving important communications such as letters and emails. A bonus is being able to retrieve important attachments such as flyers, RC Petitions, meeting attendance sheets, employee lists, and org charts. Note to politicians: at least one candidate's career was sunk by destroying correspondence.

37. Include Retired Members

Some retired members remain active participants in their unions by serving on Welfare Committees and Retiree Clubs. Their experience and their familiarity with the union make them excellent participants. Encourage retired members to get involved by attending union picnics and other events.

38. Keep Meetings Brief

A good rule of thumb is to keep meetings brief, under 60 minutes. Anything longer is probably a waste of participant's time. Leave people inspired and energized. This can be controversial to some. They don't realize how valuable people's time is and therefore, have no qualms wasting it. When we have a written agenda, and stick to the topic, we don't need to.

39. Identify Leaders Early

Look for leaders who have earned their coworker's respect and include them in the organizing campaign from the start. Their work is among the best and their work ethic strong. People trust a leader who is competent and willing to get their hands dirty. If you don't know who the leaders in the group are, just ask…

Do be aware leaders sometimes change sides during an organizing campaign. Management knows who the strongest personalities are. Supervisors focus their energy trying to win over these same individuals with promises of raises and promotions. It's not necessarily a disaster when management is successful in turning a leader, but it can make things difficult.

40. Translate Literature

Provide workers with translated materials in the language they are most comfortable with. These may include; flyers, handouts, union agreements, bylaws, constitutions and wage information, etc. Have materials checked by a trusted member familiar with the language before distributing. Taking the extra step of including translated materials will help gain support and trust. Management often overlooks such details. Be the first to translate literature and if management finally comes around they will be perceived to be following your lead.

When scheduling an initial meeting with workers ask if anyone attending will prefer handouts to be translated. If so, bring adequate quantities for workers attending, their family members, and coworkers who might be unavailable at the time.

41. Seventy Percent for Success

Although the National Labor Relations Board will allow you to file a Representation Petition with only 30 percent representation cards signed; 70 percent is proven to be the magic number for winning elections. 68 percent is close, but it's probably a loss. 69.3 percent means you've got more work to do. Remember that national campaign that went down in flames and it was in all the papers? They didn't have 70 percent of cards signed. They filed too early, planning to make up for it in the end by bringing in organizers from other states. We all saw how that ended.

42. Learn about Great Labor Leaders

Get inspired by studying the lives of those amazing labor leaders whose shoulders we stand on today. People like Mother Jones, Cesar Chavez, Harry Bridges, George Meany, Jimmy Hoffa, Henry Miller, Samuel Gompers, David Dubinsky, A. Philip Randolph, John L. Lewis, Walter Reuther, Tom Mann, and Eugene Debs all played a part in labor's history.

At the George Meany Center/National Labor College, I met a student who worked as a Teamster. The class was over for the day, so he decided to go to Washington DC by train and visit the International Brotherhood of Teamsters Office. He invited me along, but I declined. Later that night we were in the student lounge drinking beer. He pulled something out of his wallet to show me. It was General President, James P. Hoffa's business card. Written on the back in handwriting it read, "Show this brother respect. James P. Hoffa." Although I'm not a Teamster, I recognized the value of having that card.

43. Control Your Emotions

A big step toward maturity and employability is learning to control our own emotions. People who hold grudges or fly off the handle often find themselves in trouble. Saying the wrong thing in anger, getting in shouting matches or even physical altercations are examples of not controlling one's emotions. It can be with co-workers, members, family or employers. Imagine trying to negotiate a first contract, when someone on the team flies-off-the-handle throwing something across the room. Or attending a staff meeting and someone gets angry and loses it pushing a coworker out of a seat. You carpool with a coworker and they cut someone off in a road-rage incident.

The good news is, there's plenty of resources out there for people who struggle controlling their emotions. There are techniques for breathing and replacing negative thoughts. These may help us feel calm and more in control. There are books and classes, some of which may be covered by our health insurance. If we are someone who needs to work on controlling our emotions, the effort must be made.

A very conservative older secretary took offense to the way a younger secretary was dressed. For the next half-hour or so she went from cubicle-to-cubicle sharing her dislike for the young woman's dress. When no one seemed to share her concern, she became angrier. "She's a slut!" she shouted at the top of her lungs just as the young woman stepped in the door. Everyone was shocked. Realizing she was the subject of the outburst, the younger secretary suddenly stopped, turned and walked out. The rest of us followed. The tension in that office was toxic.

44. Set Big Goals for Yourself

We should all set big goals for ourselves. The bigger the goal, the greater it challenges us to become something more than we are. Goals need to be attainable, written down, with a date for a deadline.

45. Write Down Your Plan

Creating a written plan involves a bit of work, but we soon discover that it's well worth the effort. Without putting it in writing, or an alternate format, our chances of achieving our goal is slim at best. But writing it down and referring to it often will keep us focused, moving us closer and closer to the goal each day. It helps us decide where to focus our energy and how to best use our time. Even if we later decide to revise our plan, the fact that we have one will help us use the time to our advantage. Reading a plan daily is sure to keep one on track. Read it in the morning and again before bedtime.

The Power of a Written Plan

One day when I was in the eighth or ninth grade, I walked into the store and discovered that one of my classmates – a kid my age – was running the shoe department. I couldn't believe he was making an adult salary while I was recycling bottles to get spare change for an Abba-Zabba. I immediately asked him how he did it, and his answer was a wake-up call for me.

His secret was simple. Young as he was, this kid had a plan... and it wasn't selling shoes for the rest of his life. His next step was to go to Notre Dame where he would play football and study finance. He eventually did, attending college on a scholarship and pursuing the next steps of his plan. Today he's a successful investor who manages money for institutions and charitable organizations.

My friend is living proof of the power of having a plan. Just as we wouldn't build a building without a set of blueprints, we'll be able to build a more satisfying career with a written plan. Plans can change, but having a few thoughts recorded can create an edge in making successful choices.

46. Focus on Winning Elections

Make a conscious effort to direct your activities toward winning NLRB elections. Spend your time building relationships and connecting with workers who will be voting to go union. Opt-out of unrelated activities union organizers partake in that have little to do with winning NLRB elections. There are organizers who seem to make a career attending meetings; staff gatherings, job bids, port authority, city council, school board, county board of supervisors, just to name a few. There are organizers involved in dispatching union members from the hall. There are organizers involved in politics on state and national level. Some organizers have, "Organizer/Business Representative" on their business card. If this is confusing for you, imagine how members must feel. The two jobs seem to require different skill sets. Union organizers are often considered recruiters reaching out to the unrepresented, while business representatives often solve job-related disputes for members working under a union contract. I've often wondered how an "organizer/business representative" allocates his or her time. It would seem servicing current dues-paying members would rightfully win out in most situations. What percentage of time would that leave for union organizing or more specifically winning elections? As you can see, the list of distractions goes on and on. It's up to the individual to make focusing on winning NLRB elections a priority.

47. Avoid Gossip

"Those who guard their mouths and their tongues keep themselves from calamity." – Proverbs 21:23

Gossip can destroy friendships and end careers. It's often intended to elevate one person's status at the expense of another. We don't have to participate in it. If we recognize gossip for what it is, we can put an end to it.

48. Be Trustworthy

What makes someone trustworthy? We are trustworthy when we have good character and integrity. We don't have ulterior motives and are compassionate. People know they can confide in us because our actions match what we say. Be trustworthy and attract workers to the union.

49. Be Innovative

To be innovative requires us to disrupt our normal tendencies. An innovative person thinks creatively and blazes a new trail. There's a certain amount of risk involved. It may resemble an experiment at times. The purpose is to increase efficiency by doing things differently. Innovation is provocative, exciting and inspiring. Allow time for brainstorming new ideas to break out of the routine.

50. Study Organizing

Union organizing is a subject worthy of further study. Union members and activists alike can gain knowledge and experience learning from courses taught by leaders of the labor movement. Sign up for Labor Law classes, Labor History, Grievance Handling, Collective Bargaining, Arbitration, Parliamentary Procedure, Union Organizing, etc. Cornell University, Industrial and Labor Relations offers labor education courses and webinars. Some community colleges and trade schools offer labor courses. Earn a degree or certificate, or just widen your knowledge of relevant topics.

While studying for my bachelor's degree in labor studies at the George Meany Center/National Labor College, the professor informed the class that "union organizing" wasn't "faith-based", it was "science-based." She went on to say that faith and hope were great things, but they have no place in union organizing. According to the professor, every effort needs to be analyzed to see if it produced a clearly measured result. There needs to be strict parameters and proven examples. She advocated comparative case studies to measure the outcome of scientific approaches to determine whether they support the hypothesis. If not, Labor needs to throw that organizing model out and try something entirely new.

While I agree that Labor needs to be able to measure success, like a business measures return-on-investment, there seems to be so much more at play. Perhaps it's because I consider myself a person of faith. As a practicing Catholic, I believe organizing is a fulfillment of my destiny. It's about dignity of work, establishing trust and empowering people. The simple fact that we are reaching out to help people succeed, whether it be in their personal career or in growing their company, means we are already on a path to success. We cannot fail. Therefore, I recommend the following:

- Learn what other successful union organizers are doing.

- Ask them to share with you what they have learned.

- Choose what works for you.

- Put the fundamentals into practice.

- Share what you have learned with others.

In an annual job review, it was suggested that I take another course in labor law. At first, it seemed like it would be a drag, having already taken several similar courses. Up to the challenge, however, I signed-up for one being put on through LA Trade Technical College. A coworker and I found ourselves attending the same class. The instructor is a famous labor attorney who regularly charges hundreds of dollars per hour. He is a fascinating character. His precedent-setting cases have helped workers throughout the country. Teaching the short course through the local community college was his way of giving back to the labor movement. The way he saw it, he had a passion for standing up for worker's rights and if he could teach others to do the same all the better. Each evening class gave my coworker and I an opportunity to ask legal questions related to the campaigns we were working on. By semester's end, we had asked dozens of questions consulting with the top attorney in the business. It dawned on us how minimal the course fee was in relation to the valuable information provided by the instructor. On the last night of class, he bought a dozen or so pizzas which he had delivered for an end of semester celebration. That was proof to me what he wasn't doing it for the money.

51. Know Why Workers Join Unions

The following is a list of 101 reasons workers join unions. You may be able to identify others. If so, please feel free to contact the author. Pay attention to the top 10 reasons, as you'll often hear these referred to by union organizers. Keep in mind everyone has their own motivations. There may be a combination of many reasons that convince a person to seek union representation and a better way of life.

101 Reasons to Join a Union

1) Wages - Union workers earn 15% more than non-union employees

2) Paid Vacations - Union workers have 28% more paid vacations

3) Pension - Union workers have 386% more defined-benefit pension plans

4) Disability Insurance - Union workers have 77% more short term disability insurance

5) Better safety training – Right to address safety concerns

6) Solidarity - Brotherhood

7) Job Security

8) Grievance Procedures

9) Weingarten rights – Right to have representative present during questioning

10) Representation

11) Strength in numbers – More power as a group

12) Learn a Trade

12) State Certification training

13) Improve skills

14) Apprentice opportunities (Classes and Books paid)

15) 401K Plan

16) Family Medical

17) Training

18) Health benefits (Free Prescriptions, safety glasses, body scan, etc.)

19) Local hiring

20) Nationwide job location service

21) Skill upgrade programs

22) Death benefits

23) Respect in the workplace -

24) Collective Bargaining – No more embarrassment asking for a raise/Pay disparity

25) Overtime benefits

26) Contractor classes ($5000 bonus after 1st year of business)

27) Work under a written contract

28) Raise standard of living

29) Endless Upward Mobility

30) Protection of worker's rights

31) Apprenticeship Training

32) Journeyman training

33) Legal protection

34) Hands on training (On the job) Earn while you learn

35) Scholarships

36) Teaching opportunities (Apprenticeship, etc.)

37) Right to strike

39) Vote where to allocate raises

39) Vote on who represents you

40) Ability to run for office

41) Contract Survey - Be involved in making recommendations for future negotiations

42) Some union dues are tax deductible

43) Health Plan Advocate – Helps members navigate the health plan

44) Recognition as industry leader – Gain recognition by joining the best

45) Access to Prevailing Wage Projects

46) Standby pay – Also known as on-call pay when employer restricts worker's free time

47) Negotiated Tool List (Less tools to provide because the contractor is responsible to provide)

48) Overtime Wage Opportunities

49) Union discounts on tools and boots

50) Steward on job -

51) Division of Overtime - Overtime distributed evenly

52) Age Consideration Clause (Over 50 Rule)

53) Publications updating you of opportunities throughout country

54) Journeyman ticket recognized in other jurisdictions

55) Portable skills used worldwide

56) Civil Service Opportunities (ie: 5 agencies Los Angeles) Government work

57) Right to due process (Discipline)

58) Pride in craftsmanship

59) Do it right the first time

60) Continue training as new fields open up

61) Local Hiring Agreements – work in own jurisdiction

62) Higher Standards (ie: Apprenticeship Standards)

63) Written Career Plan (Plan for success)

64) Special Skill Wage

65) Foreman Call Out by Name (Dispatch)

66) Out of Work List – Ease of collecting unemployment/ No more job interviews

67) Reverse Lay Off

68) Weekly pay – if check is late receive overtime pay

69) Member Assistance Program – Mental health assistance for members

70) Use of vehicles clause – Keeps employer from relying on your vehicle for company purposes.

71) Drug and Alcohol Policy – Testing reduces risk of accidents and violence

72) Signs required on Trucks – Magnetic signs not allowed/ your vehicle is not company truck

73) Holiday Pay – Set in contract

74) Show-Up Pay – Aka reporting pay for showing-up as scheduled, when no work is available.

75) Foreman Call Out by Name – Guarantees wage rate for set period of time

76) Apprentice Skills Competition – Win prizes/trips/receive recognition

77) Perfect Attendance Award – Receive recognition for being reliable

78) Payroll and Fringe Benefits Guarantee Trust Fund – Pays if company goes bankrupt

79) Banked hours in medical plan – up to 6 months!!!

80) Membership Orientation Class – Helps new members assimilate/answers questions

81) Access to PLA jobs – Require hiring through union

82) A Voice in the Workplace -

83) Alternative Pathways to Becoming Journeyman -

84) Transitional Agreement – Allows for smooth transition into union over time

85) Job Placement -

86) Emergency Work List – Available in case of disaster, floods, earth quakes, fires

87) FSA Debit Card – Flexible Spending Account debit card for medical out-of-pocket expenses

88) Vote on contract -

89) Apprenticeship Graduation Ceremony – Author's was a black-tie affair on the Queen Mary

90) Join a Movement – The labor movement fights for worker's rights every day

91) Dignity – No more walking on egg shells thinking you'll be fired for arbitrary reasons

92) Sick Leave -

93) Clear Policies – Written in a way as to not be vague or left to interpretation by management

94) Fair Treatment – A harmonious workplace where you are less vulnerable to job loss

95) Tuition Reimbursement -

96) Participate in Social Activities – To improve work life balance

97) Health and Welfare Committee – Volunteers to pay your union dues if sick or injured

98) Death benefits for heirs

99) Comfort the Family – Representatives attend memorial service and comforts family

100) Share Similar Values -

101) Moment of silence – members memorialized at union meeting/charter draped in black cloth in tribute for a period of 30 days.

102) Community Outreach

52. Know Your Benefits Package

Do you know how your benefits package compares to the competition? How much are the copays for the medical plan? How many kids can be covered? Be ready to answer future member's questions as well as employers. There's usually a transitional period from the time the non-union employer's insurance runs out and the union's kicks-in. Often you can work out with the insurer so workers will not be stuck without coverage. Find out so you know in advance. There can be a distinct advantage to having an organizer with experience having served as a health plan trustee. There are many nuances as to how both employers and employees transition into the union's medical plan.

53. Study the Collective Bargaining Agreement

Do you know your Collective Bargaining Agreement inside-and-out? You should be able to find topics quickly and be able to explain parts of the agreement to members and employers. Having a thorough understanding of the collective bargaining agreement will help in deflecting unwarranted criticism. Pay attention to meal periods and overtime rules. These are the areas where employer's often get themselves in trouble.

54. Know the State and Federal Minimum Wage

The Fair Labor Standards Act determines what the minimum wage is for private and public-sector employees. If you haven't looked at your State and Federal Minimum Wage Rates lately you might be in for quite a surprise. Employers don't always replace minimum wage posters as required by Law.

55. Share the Credit

Winning takes teamwork. Acknowledge each person's contribution. Have you ever been a small part of a victory and had your name mentioned? It feels great! Ever worked your ass off and somehow, they forgot to mention you? Ouch! You work day-after-day, putting in long hours sometimes skipping meals only to have some knucklehead forget you were there. That sucks! Seasoned politicians almost never do this. They go out of their way to make a list and thank every individual no matter how insignificant their role. When they get to the end of their list, they ask the crowd if they are forgetting anyone. Inevitably, a voice will call out their own name and the politician will backtrack and say, "how silly of me! of course, how could I have forgotten (fill in the blank)?" That's how they keep from alienating their own constituents. People love them for it!

A very successful friend of mine in the labor movement has a gift for making others feel good about themselves. His stellar career has launched him to the top, but he refuses to acknowledge his own successes and instead focuses on others. That combination of quick wit and self-deprecating humor is infectious. Share the credit with everyone.

56. Avoid Spiking the Ball

Accept wins graciously. Celebrate victories, but don't rub it in anybody's face. It's tempting, but here's an opportunity to prove we are professional. We're sure to lose a few campaigns ourselves. Trust me, it hurts.

We lost a campaign at a small shop. The election took place in their office on payday. The first clue things weren't going well was none of the workers looked us in the face. They were out in the parking lot waiting for their paychecks. We knew then it would be a loss. As we walked out the door after the count, one of the office personnel couldn't help but take a jab at us. In a thick Russian accent, she said, "it's an international tragedy for you guys." The company owner told her to chill, in Russian of course. I kind of respect that guy for not gloating.

57. Dress to Impress

Be the professional union organizer everyone wants to work with. Always try to look your best.

Dress for The Organizing Position You Want

First impressions stick, so look good. Find out how organizers in your industry tend to dress and turn it up a notch. Help people visualize you in the position you want. We each have our own style and tastes, but there are general guidelines you can pick up from others if you pay attention. If there is any question about what an organizer is expected to wear in your industry; do some research or ask. Make a mental note of what other organizers tend to wear by observing them.

58. Ditch the Golf Clubs

Don't transport golf clubs in the trunk of your car. Don't have a putter in your office (even for security). If you do, eventually someone is going to assume this is how you spend your days when you should be working.

We were given an assignment to round up members for a city council meeting. Dispatch was just finishing up at the hall. Several members agreed to volunteer when we dangled the carrot of a free meal afterwards. Parking would be expensive at city hall, so we carpooled. One of the organizers offered to drive. While moving items from the backseat to the trunk one of the members eyed a set of golf clubs. The whole drive downtown, they joked about the clubs in the trunk, and how we probably wished we were out golfing. We took quite a ribbing that day.

59. Embrace Chaos

There will be times when you are absolutely slammed. Learn to enjoy a crazy, hectic schedule. You'll find that multiple appointments and back-to-back meetings will stretch you in ways you've never thought of.

Something came up and a representative couldn't attend a meeting with the University of California, Compliance and Audit Committee. Instead of canceling, someone came up with the idea of sending me, a rookie organizer at the time. Six weeks earlier I was running pipe at the Metro Rail as an electrician. It wasn't clear what any of this had to do with organizing. The union had a problem with a nonunion contractor who was eating our lunch. That much was clear. How could someone like me, convince the Board of Regents not to allow a contractor to bid on a multimillion dollar project?

I was given a file and sent me on my way. There wasn't enough time to get acclimated with the project. The meeting was about to begin. The committee members were very cordial, but it was clear they made their mind up before the meeting began. Still, I got a few jabs in and let them know we weren't going to roll-over. We were going to hold them personally responsible for safety violations and cost overruns. The community would be up-in-arms over every deviation. It was going to haunt them for their entire careers. It was rather enjoyable. Was I in over my head? Absolutely, without a doubt. Did they have subsequent meetings to keep the contractor in-line? You better believe it. Mission accomplished.

On another occasion, there was a meeting scheduled with a dozen or so water district workers. We were to meet at a pizza parlor in the high desert. My role was to be there to support the local union organizer. It was going to be an easy evening. Show up, meet some workers, eat some pizza, and be home by midnight. It wasn't clear from the email; what water district the workers were from. It just said to be there at 6 pm and the organizer would brief me. At 6 pm, he hadn't arrived yet. There were workers waiting near the door. The wind was blowing so hard we decided to go inside. The organizer wasn't answering his phone. The manager of the restaurant was busy clearing an area for us. She informed us the highway was closed. There was an overturned tanker truck blocking all lanes. Some of her workers couldn't get through. The organizer called to say he would be late. It was up to me to run the meeting. Instead of 15 water district workers there were over 50 spread out in two rooms. Mixed in between were some families having dinner. We started a tab, ordered drinks, appetizers, pizzas, and salads. In my trunk were some clipboards and miscellaneous union literature. We got a sign-in sheet going around. The organizer called to say he had cards for everyone to sign, but he was still an hour out. Luckily, there was a box of blank representation cards in my trunk. People were hitting me with questions; one-after-another. There were multiple people talking in English and in Spanish. Somehow, we got everyone fed, the cards were signed and questions answered. When the local union organizer arrived, there wasn't much for him to do but grab a beer and have a seat. Most of the workers, had already left satisfied. From chaos comes growth. Embrace it!

60. Put Your Ego in Check

An inflated ego can block a person's ability to communicate effectively. It can make a person unteachable and lead to conflict. Our need to be right can complicate even the simplest tasks making us hard to supervise. Western culture doesn't always value introspection and self-reflection. Many people have come to realize, there's value in getting to know ourselves better. The reward for self-reflection is emotional health. While it can take years to construct our self-images, we're capable of analyzing ourselves in a few hours. Finding healthy balances between arrogance and humility, confidence and insecurity, will lead to better communication and relationships. Changing bad habits might take time, but identifying them is a healthy first step.

61. Admit Your Mistakes

All of us make them, yet none of us want to admit it. We screwed up! Everyone knows it. Now let's take that error and learn from it. Own it! We're one-step-closer to success and ready to move on. See how easy that was?

The news reported on a once-in-lifetime phenomenon called a "Super Bloom," taking place in Death Valley, California. It's a condition causing wildflowers to suddenly bloom in an arid desert due to excessive rain. Having already requested the week off from work, it seemed like a great vacation idea. My then seven-year-old son and I found a rugged camping spot at Wildrose in Death Valley National Park.

The next day we headed out for a drive. We traveled clear across the valley to Scotty's Castle, a popular tourist destination. There we hiked, took a guided tour, and picnicked under a tree which are rare in that area. Before we knew it, the sun was going down. We needed to get back to the campground. It was getting darker and darker. The road was unrecognizable from just a few hours earlier. It seemed like we were the only car on the road for miles at a time. I turned left at a fork in the road, but my son said, "turn right." I was sure he was mistaken. An hour later, we approached a sign that read, "Welcome to Nevada. The Silver State." I spun the car around and tried to distract my son. He wasn't fooled. "See?" he said. "I was right."

62. Encourage Workers to Keep Daily Journals

Composition notebooks where the pages cannot easily be torn out are perfect. Ask the worker to sign and date each page and include notes about conversations with management, happenings as well as weather conditions and break times. The journal could become invaluable if the worker gets fired, is a witness or is involved in a lawsuit. Anything that helps an employee remember specifics can be helpful. You could spend time explaining what a composition notebook looks like, or you could just buy one and give it to the worker. Problem solved.

It takes a certain amount of determination and self-control to write in a journal consistently. The person must be motivated. Talk in terms of a potential lawsuit. They'll understand what you are saying.

Supervisors are often tasked with similar responsibilities to protect the company from litigation. Work is tracked and employee's absences, verbal warnings, accidents and such are recorded. While running a crew for an electrical contractor in Los Angeles, the company had us Foreman complete a daily job journal. We were more interested in protecting ourselves than the company and worded everything accordingly.

The project began to fall behind schedule. We were told to fudge the numbers. In other words, instead of tracking our crew as installing underground conduit, we were to report the work as hallway lighting. No one felt comfortable about it and we protested. An emergency meeting was called in the project manager's trailer. All the foremen were present. The job was way behind schedule. According to the project management program, the foundation should have been poured and the walls erected. We were still working in the dirt, but the project manager insisted we were to fill out the paperwork as if we were on schedule.

One day the CEO and an entourage flew out from New York for a surprise visit. They were expecting to see a completed building but instead found only a frame. A short time later the project manager walked out of the trailer with a cardboard box under his arm. He was terminated. They escorted him to the gate. We all thought we would be next. Somehow, we dodged a bullet. The project ran smoothly after that.

63. Avoid Using Jargon

Brain surgery is complicated. Union organizing is relatively simple. Avoid using jargon when speaking with members and workers about organizing. Labor attorneys and college professors seem fascinated with terms like; common situs picketing, Moore Drydock Standards, hot cargo clauses, intervenors, exclusive bargaining rights, and zipper clauses. Most people's eyes glaze over at the mention of just one of these phrases. Industry jargon tends to complicate communication.

64. Write a Letter to the Editor

Writing a letter to the editor of a newspaper can get your topic noticed by activists, members of the public, and elected officials. Even if it's not published, the issue has been submitted for consideration to the editorial department. As more letters are received on the issue, it's more likely to be examined by the editorial staff. Many union organizers, for good reasons, don't trust the press or media. They may have had experiences where an interview by a reporter went south or caused trouble. A well-written letter to the editor of a newspaper is a safer bet. Keep in mind if chosen for publishing, a letter to the editor might appear in-whole or reduced in length, with or without a response. Keep to the publication's guidelines when submitting letters. Respond quickly, within a day or two to a specific article by title, date, and author to be considered for publishing. If you have certain qualifications as an expert, include this information in the letter.

While serving as an apprentice electrician building the Metrorail subway in Los Angeles, I became alarmed at the negative press the project was getting. According to the papers, there was little demand for a subway in Los Angeles. A popular radio host speculated that shortly after the project was completed it would be filled with sand and abandoned. People just couldn't fathom commuters in Los Angeles riding a subway. Newspapers demanded a more conservative approach to add buses along the route. They said a subway would only attract criminals, and be impossible for police to patrol. Next, they complained about the cost overruns and businesses being affected. Then they attacked the union workers as being lazy. I had enough. I penned a blistering response. The next morning, I double checked it for errors and sent it to the editor. To my amazement, it was printed it in its entirety. Every scathing word from my poison pen placed precisely like a claymore mine ready to detonate. When I got to class the instructor said, "Wow! You really gave it to that guy." My parents called to tell me they saw my letter in the newspaper. When the project finally opened, they had to add extra railcars because ridership was almost twice what they had projected. Twenty-five years later, the Metro Red Line carries 149,096 passengers a day, 817,000,000 total passengers or 3.6 billion miles.

65. Find Consensus

It's not easy to get a group to agree, but allowing everyone a chance to speak and be heard increases our odds. Consensus can be defined as an acceptable solution. Harmony in a group can mean the difference between winning and losing.

66. Identify Allies

Look for like-minded unions, associations, and community groups to form alliances with. We don't have to agree on every issue. Identify common ground where working together makes sense.

67. Act on Intuition

There's a certain feeling we get, where we must trust our gut and act on intuition. Perhaps it's solving a perceived problem without all the information, or maybe it's more than that. It has been described as the hair standing up on the back of your neck. We just know. Some people seem more intuitive than others. Are they just lucky or do they pay better attention than others? Is it possible to learn intuition or at least nurture it?

In extreme situations, it's the person who liquidates their portfolio days before a stock market crash averting financial ruin. In another case, it's a person canceling a flight because of a feeling, only to find out later the plane crashed. In sales, it might be someone visualizing a red carpet and two trumpeters welcoming them to the door of a prospect. With that positive of a feeling, who could fail?

My great grandmother wrote all her grown kids and asked them to come home for Thanksgiving. This was during the Great Depression. My Grandfather was unemployed living out of state. His wife (my grandmother) encouraged him to go, though traveling expenses would cause great hardship. The family gathered at my great grandmother's farm and had a wonderful Thanksgiving meal. After dinner, she excused herself to take a nap while her kids cleaned the dishes. She went upstairs and died in her sleep.

68. Enjoy the Journey

Stop to take stock from time-to-time. Notice how far you've come to this point. Our careers are what we make of them. We've chosen union organizing as our vocation. It's not just the destination that is satisfying, it's the journey. Enjoy yourself.

69. Learn about Neutrality Agreements

With a neutrality agreement, the employer agrees to remain neutral, with regards to the union organizing its workforce. The agreement might bar the company from conducting captive audience meetings with employees and include "card check" or other provisions. As some organizers have discovered, employers don't always honor neutrality agreements.

A campaign with a multinational company, resulted in a neutrality agreement when it was discovered there was a similar agreement with a union in Europe. In an act of solidarity, leaders of the union overseas wrote a letter to the CEO demanding the company remain neutral in its dealings with the union effort in America. A copy of the neutrality agreement and solidarity letter were helpful when meeting with workers.

70. Be Teachable

"When the student is ready the teacher will appear. When the student is truly ready… The teacher will disappear." - Lao Tzu

To be teachable we need to be humble. There's no room for arrogance. We need to be like a sponge and allow new ideas to be absorbed into the mind.

The first few weeks of my apprenticeship were a blur. Prior to getting accepted into the union, I worked nonunion under-the-table. It was impossible to prove the hours without paystubs. At the time, I was convinced the union was screwing me for not crediting me with prior experience. My journeyman tried to convince me otherwise, but I wouldn't listen. He finally gave-in urging me to challenge their assessment by taking a hands-on test. The result? It was a humbling experience. I found out I acquired some bad habits that needed to be forgotten and quick. At work the next day, I was ready to listen. That's when the apprenticeship really began.

71. Be Reliable

Workers who contact the union for help, expect us to be reliable. If we schedule a meeting they trust us to show up on time and do what we say we are going to do. We must prove we are reliable. There's no room for flakes in union organizing.

72. Take Pride in Your Work

Walk proud and know your efforts will make a difference in the world. The industry begs for passionate, caring individuals who take pride in their work. Those who do will be rewarded and remembered.

An admired organizer recently announced his retirement at a meeting. He choked-up as he informed the group of his decision. The emotions caught him off-guard as much as it did us. He recalled his early days working as an organizer, the first in his local, getting to know the jurisdiction, and "making it up on the fly" as he described. Others chimed-in with similar memories, congratulating him on a job-well-done. He mentioned other union organizers, who were gone now but were every bit as influential to his career. We knew the names and concurred, they were exceptional.

73. Create Good Luck

"Chance favors a prepared mind." – Louis Pasteur

Action precedes good fortune. Bad luck is often a result of inaction or lack of proper planning. We can create good luck by bouncing back from failure and never quitting. Say it aloud often:

- I feel lucky

- People around me are lucky

- Good things always happen to me

74. Think BIGGER

"Whatever you can do, or dream you can do, begin it. Boldness has genius, power, and magic in it. Begin it now." – Johann Wolfgang von Goethe

Why put limits on our thinking? We've got one life to live and a billion possibilities for outcomes. Where would we be now if the founders of our great unions thought small-scale. From now on think BIGGER.

75. Know When to Say "No"

Choose targets and assignments carefully. Know when to say "no." Every effort takes a certain amount of emotional energy. Don't risk your health, relationships or mental stability by taking on too many tasks at one time. Some campaigns need time to germinate.

76. Validate Other's Feelings

"Instruction does much, but encouragement does everything." - Johann Wolfgang von Goethe

We all have different backgrounds, experiences, and beliefs. The way we share emotions make us unique. We validate people's feelings by not judging and letting them know they are understood. We do this by showing genuine empathy, taking time to listen completely, and avoiding giving advice unless asked.

77. Believe in Your Ability

"Keep your fears to yourself, but share your courage with others." - Robert Louis Stevenson

Union organizers are great communicators, with talents and abilities perfectly suited for leadership roles. Your ability to recruit new union members make you a valuable member of any team. Believe in yourself!

78. Talk Past, Present, Future

Practice this technique for those times when we get tongue tied and aren't sure what to say. Toastmaster's practice speaking on what they call, "table topics" a question posed out of the blue. They are required to speak on a random question for three minutes. There's bound to be time in every union organizer's career where they are called to the mic and asked to speak on a given topic. Using this formula, we start with the past. Once that is covered, we discuss the topic in present tense. Then we move on to the future and wrap it up. Use this technique when tongue-tied.

79. Give People a Chance to Respond

Some of the best trainers, pause for a moment and ask, "does that make sense?" They're looking for feedback to see if the audience is paying attention and understands the concepts. If someone looks puzzled or says, "you lost me," a good trainer will double back and go over the part in question again. This helps both the student and the trainer refine the lesson.

This concept of giving people a chance to respond can be used in a variety of ways, not just the classroom. Business has mastered this idea by using surveys to gauge the quality of customer service. The fact that a company asks for feedback, sometimes makes us feel better. We get a chance to let someone know of a problem and air our complaint. Woe to the business that doesn't ask for feedback, they won't know when they've got a problem.

Some union halls have incorporated the idea by installing a "suggestion box." It's an anonymous way for members to make recommendations to staff.

In union organizing, we have face-to-face meetings, house calls, surveys, votes, elections, and more. All are designed to empower workers and allow people a chance to respond.

80. Celebrate the Wins

The best advice given to me when I first began organizing, was to celebrate the wins. The truth is, they can be few and far between. This means finding some way to celebrate victories with our members and taking time to acknowledge and report on everyone's efforts. I recommend such things as celebrating anniversary dates for the founding of an organizing committee, local, or opening of a training facility. Throwing a party for volunteers after a successful campaign can have a rejuvenating effect on everyone involved. It helps us avoid burning out and overworking staff or volunteers.

There is a tendency to brush aside one successful campaign and jump right onto another target without taking the time to recognize individual's contributions.

Educate members about recent accomplishments

- Build consensus on what works and what doesn't

- Report at meetings

- Share videos and photos

- Welcome new members

- Have a celebration

- Serve cake at meetings

81. Mention Your Clients

You had some stellar successes, signed contractors and attracted new members into the union. They've gone on to make a good life for themselves and their families. Don't keep those stories a secret, mention your clients. Give people examples they can emulate. Use inspiring stories to encourage accomplishment.

82. Action Beats Planning

Stuck in a rut? Bored? Take action to get things moving. Put some of the ideas you've gained from reading this book to work in your union. Almost immediately you'll notice progress. It's not that complicated. The labor movement along with countless organizations and institutions has a glaring problem. Too much time wasted in planning meetings and conferences that drag on hour after countless hour. It's as if someone is saying, "let's pull our most talented people out of the field to talk about organizing." How has that worked out? Huge swaths of the country have seen membership reductions, budget constraints and employers going non-union. Boredom starts at the top and oozes down through the fiber of the whole operation until even the rank-and-file member finds the idea of another meeting detestable. The worst part, some are doing it on purpose! If no one shows up, there's less competition for leadership positions.

A decertification effort by members of a local union was in progress. The international union was notified just two weeks prior to the election. An appointment with the business manager followed. The moment the reps walked into the office they recognized the problem. The place looked like a museum. The business manager was a die-cast car collector. Everywhere, the walls, the desk, a conference table, were beautifully displayed die-cast cars most still in original boxes. The effort involved in carefully placing each car, each shelf perfectly aligned from floor to ceiling, must have been very time-consuming. Before getting down to business he gave a tour. There was the first die-cast car ever bought. Then there were examples of cars his family had owned and a model truck resembling the one in the parking lot. It was an impressive collection. Only someone retired would have enough time on their hands to amass such a collection. We weren't interested in the grand tour. We needed to get busy knocking on member's doors to convince them to stay with the union, but first, he insisted on a planning meeting.

Another local union appeared to be struggling. Reps were sent to a planning meeting. The local needed to increase membership quick to avoid being insolvent. Arriving at the address, they wondered if it was the right location. It seemed more like a suite in a quiet medical building than a union hall. They walked in, noticed a huge union logo on a red wall. Yes, they had found the place. There were two folding tables set up with conference chairs, a coffee pot and a kitchenette. One of the two small offices to the left was used for storage the other the business manager's office with a bathroom to the right. The secretary had a small desk near the door. The entire operation was visible from where they stood.

After pleasantries, the attendees sat down and the meeting began. The business manager started by informing everyone if he didn't get new members soon, he would be forced to let the secretary go. This was said within earshot of the secretary. She looked up for a second but didn't seem particularly surprised. He went on to say no members attend the monthly meetings. It's too far from where they work. They don't want to get involved. The workers are mostly Republican and don't share the union's politics. The past administration soured relationships with the employer. Many actionable recommendations were made, all of which were ignored. There were several additional follow-up meetings, but nothing much ever transpired. These became an annual event. Afterwards, they would go to a restaurant and have lunch together before the long drive home. The secretary was let go. It didn't matter because in all the times they met at the office the phone never rang. So, they would go through the motions. They would meet and confer. If the recommendations were adopted the local might grow, but everyone knew it was never going to happen.

83. Find Time to Exercise

Some people never exercise. It's a shame. They sit for hours a day on-the-job hardly getting up to stretch and wonder why they feel like crap. They may never know the satisfaction gained at the end of a strenuous workout. Ever walked out of a gym drenched in sweat feeling ten-feet-tall? That's the endorphins kicking-in. We think to ourselves, "I feel great! why not do this every day?" The excuse used most often for not exercising is lack of time, but we all have the same amount. It's all about priorities. The trick is to focus on the results we want.

Everyone wants to be healthy and fit. Millions of dollars are spent on magazines in grocery lines touting the perfect body, flat abs, bigger arms. Those are great aspirations, but most people would be satisfied to have more energy and sleep better at night. Whatever our goals are, we must make them attainable. Look for ways to squeeze in an exercise routine. Throw a gym bag in the trunk with some walking shoes for those times when you arrive at a destination early. Put some dumbbells in the office. Do some curls during breaks. A gym membership is a great investment. Try to find a national chain for those times you are on-the-road. Take advantage of the weight rooms, the machines, cardio classes, pool, and jacuzzi. Hotel workout rooms vary in quality, but most offer cardio machines and free weights. The trick is to change up the routine enough that you don't get bored. Stay hydrated. Use the free wipes to clean the equipment and avoid getting sick. When we feel better we're more effective on-the-job.

84. Make Incremental Improvements

Often, to be the best all a person needs to do is be a little better than the next guy. It's the extra little improvements we make that add up over time. Everything we do can be improved upon in some manner. Analyze your activities the way a coach would with the mindset of this isn't good enough. Then go about making adjustments.

85. Put Your Toes in the Sand

Every now and then we need to walk away from union organizing and enjoy the weekend with our friends and family. Funny thing is, when we do, we're more focused and effective upon our return. The trick is keeping the right balance between work and recreation. Most successful people work six days a week. That's six days on and one day off.

86. Throw Your Shoulders Back

Here's a quick body language tip to make yourself appear slimmer, more confident, and more attractive. Throw your shoulders back and keep your head up high as you walk into a room. This slight movement forces you to pull your stomach in.

In elementary school, the teachers were always trying to get us to sit up straight and throw our shoulders back. They were trying to show us how to engage and look more confident. If only we could go back and thank them.

A general foreman named Keith on the Metrorail Subway project exuded tremendous confidence when he walked into a room. He was like General Patton with his shoulders back and his head up high. It seemed to work for him. The company gave him a truck, a credit card and put him in charge of a crew of around 50 workers. I made a conscious effort to focus on my own posture. It takes a little practice. When we find ourselves forgetting, we have to refocus our efforts. Soon it becomes a habit, a good-habit at that.

87. Define Your Brand

If you don't define your own brand, who you are, what you do, what you stand for, someone else will. Union organizers develop all types of branding, some intentional and others not so much. There's the redneck with the ten-gallon hat, the strong silent type, the one known for dinging contractors, the boss's kid, the closer, the sandal wearing vegan, etc.

What's your specialty? What organizing activity do you do most often? What are you good at? What sets you apart from other organizers? What image, words or services do you want people to identify you with?

88. Learn from Other's Mistakes

We can learn a lot by making mistakes, but we can learn just as much watching others fail. It's much less painful, expensive and embarrassing being a bystander. Become an observer of all things messed-up. Take a "you first" approach. If someone stumbles out into the road yelling, "the bridge is out," pull over. If a coworker loses attitude and tries to get you involved. Say, "no thanks." Sometimes people get laid-off in pairs.

89. Take a Different Route

Do you drive to the office on the same route each day? Do you catch the same train at the same time each morning? Don't fall into a routine. Mix it up a bit. Doing so could reveal missed opportunities. Force yourself to change habits. This will help avoid getting caught in a rut. Sometimes a change of scenery can open our eyes to opportunities, projects, and developments taking place in the community. Be the go-to-person that people approach when anything new is happening

90. Listen to Motivational Recordings

Start each day with positive thoughts, mindfulness and a sense of gratitude to transform your career. We are a sum of the thoughts we put into our minds. Too many people pollute their thinking with somebody did someone wrong songs, worry, and fear. They wonder why they feel lousy and sluggish at work. Time spent commuting can be time invested in listening to motivational or instructional recordings to nourish our intellect. Many of the most successful intellectuals and thought leaders have published recordings to share what they have learned. It would be a shame not to utilize these valuable resources.

91. Find a Partner with Complimentary Talents

We don't always get a chance to choose who we work with, but when two union organizers with complimentary talents collaborate, output can triple even quadruple. Synergy happens when one's strengths make up for the other's weaknesses and vice-versa. Keep an eye out for someone you enjoy working with who has similar interests and values. Do some self-reflection to identify your major strengths and weaknesses. How can you best assist each other to succeed?

92. Print Meeting Agendas

Keep meeting attendees focused on items of importance by printing meeting agendas. There's a danger whenever you get a handful of people together for a meeting that it will get high jacked. Soon the productive get-together can turn into a convoluted mess. That's not supposed to happen. Print meeting agendas, and share in advance with your group. Each person can then come prepared ready to participate.

Have you ever attended a meeting that was supposed to be about one thing and it turned out to be about something entirely different? You know what a pain it can be. Meetings can drag on for hours with no direction. They're painful to sit through. There was a supervisor that had a habit of holding meetings for no apparent reason. We would talk and talk but nothing ever seemed to get accomplished. At some point, he would recognize we were starving-to-death and order food. Meetings were interrupted by phone calls, people walking in the room and any distraction you could imagine. Then he'd ask what we had been talking about. Often, no one could remember. He would either start from the top or bring up another subject. Luckily the guy had a great sense of humor. He was a natural comedian. Sometimes we wondered if he was just trying out material on us. When he left the department, we didn't have another meeting for a year. It didn't affect productivity whatsoever.

93. Use Action Items

Action items are topics discussed in a meeting that direct something to be accomplished usually by an individual. The next meeting the action item appears on the agenda. The person responsible is expected to report back on the progress.

My Dad always tells me to add action items to meeting agendas to keep people on track. It's not bad advice and since this was repeated to me hundreds of times, it's worth noting here. Dad worked as a Senior Scientist at Hughes Aircraft Company on such projects as the Lunar Surveyor and AMRAAM missile project. According to my Dad, there were people at Hughes who made a living attending meetings. They never did any work. This was always a pet-peeve of his. He combated this problem by adding action items to meeting agendas. The next meeting, he would ask how the work was progressing. It took a while before everyone in the engineering department realized, if there was an action item with their name, it had better be completed. My Dad was old school. He was serious as a heart attack.

94. Appoint a Secretary to Take Notes

When running a meeting, have someone take notes. You will want to know in the future who attended, what decisions were made, and what information was provided, what time the meeting started and ended, where it was conducted and why. You can look back at these notes and see what progress has been made.

Not everyone is interested in transcribing what happened in a meeting. Find the person who is. That person should be a good listener, well organized and thorough. When possible, find someone with a sense of humor. It will make reading minutes more entertaining.

A friend was elected secretary of a monthly meeting of union organizers. These meetings were tense at first, as tempers flared. Various organizers competed for attention. My friend's sharp wit and masterful use of sarcasm made these meetings enjoyable. Anyone else would have been fired for committing to paper what my friend did. He had an artful way of poking-fun at all the participants. He pushed right up to the edge before backing off. After each meeting, I took the minutes home to share with my Dad who was retired. He had spent years conducting business meetings during his career. Dad appreciated the witty, dead-pan humor displayed in the writing. He loved to read them.

95. Review Business Reports

A business report, such as a Dunn and Bradstreet is an overview including research and insights about companies for vendors, financial institutions, suppliers, and marketers. We can learn a great deal about a company by reviewing their business report. Some of the information available will be the approximate number of employees, financial stability, supplier risk, market forecast, etc.

96. Make a FOIA Request

The Freedom of Information Act in the US or FOIPA Freedom of Information and Privacy Act in Canada gives citizens the right to access information from the government. File a request by mail, but only after reviewing the free guide on their website at https://foia.gov .

97. Clear-In with the Local

Clear-in with the local that has jurisdiction if you are planning to meet with workers in another's area. As your reputation for helping workers grows, more individuals will reach out to you for help. You will be influencing workers outside of your jurisdiction. Some business managers are more territorial than others. Avoid getting in trouble. Build trust by keeping everyone informed of your intentions. The best bet is to include the organizer in the area.

Learn from my mistake. After receiving a call from some workers up the coast interested in union representation I made the three-hour trek. Along the route, I decided that informing the business manager of the area wasn't necessary. The chances of running into each other wasn't likely. I met with ten non-union workers at a coffee house with an outdoor patio. We pulled several tables together, repositioned umbrellas and set up a circle so everyone could hear.

The moment we sat down to introduce ourselves, the business manager of the jurisdiction walked out with a coffee cup in hand.

He took one look at us and with a surprised look on his face walked over to his car. I got up quickly and ran over to explain the situation. It was embarrassing, to say the least. He was gracious about it, but I hope to never make that mistake again. It had the potential to sour our relationship. He had a good sense of humor and laughed it off. But he reminded me, the local had an organizer who would have liked to have been involved. The truth is, the organizer might have already met with the group. There might have been information or resources already allocated. My attitude was, "Hey! It's my lead. Go get your own," but that's the wrong attitude to have.

98. Incorporate the Latest Technology

Insist on organizing with the latest technology to give yourself and the union an edge. Whether it's for performing research, word processing, tracking projects, routing or updating a database demand the most up to date tools for the job. There is no denying technology has greatly affected the way union organizing is done today and will continue to do so in the future.

Social Media

Social media allows us to connect and engage with individuals 24 hours a day, 7 days a week. These services provide opportunities to learn and compare strategies and tactics. Here are some ways you might use these services for organizing:

- Promote your union

- Advertise training opportunities

- Announce job listings

- Describe membership opportunities

- Encourage referrals

- Contact and help job seekers

- Recommend alternative career paths

- Warn job seekers of potential scams

- Engage and collaborate with members

- Publish photos and videos of union activities

The fact that so many companies use these services to market their business and products shows how important social media has become. It's an inexpensive marketing tool that if used correctly could increase referrals. More and more recruiters are relying on social networks to convince quality candidates to join their team.

99. Don't Be a Potty-Mouth

Many people in the workplace seem unaware how distasteful and downright rude their use of foul language is. Many of us have used inappropriate language from time to time, but we need to be careful. It can be considered abusive or harassment when directed at subordinates. In some situations, there can be a major liability. It's unprofessional, to say the least.

My first job as an indentured apprentice was at the Trillium building in Woodland Hills. It was three-tenths of a mile from home. They partnered me up with a journeyman they called "Chicken Frank." He got the nickname because he ate chicken every day for lunch. Frank was a great electrician, but he had a foul mouth. He would cuss constantly. He took great pleasure in making apprentices feel uncomfortable. Once, he ran into my then girlfriend's father and told him, "Hey! I'm working with your son-in-law." Her dad wasn't that fond of me and Frank knew it.

One-day Frank invited me to a Dodger game. He bought four tickets; two were for me and my girlfriend at the time, and the others for Frank and his daughter. We were to meet at the stadium that Friday night. I warned my date about Frank's language. I told her he would probably be crude and cuss like a sailor. My guess was he was going to get drunk and make an ass out of himself. To my surprise, he was a complete gentleman. Frank brought his 10-year-old daughter. The seats were in pavilion where they don't sell alcohol because Frank didn't want his daughter around any drunks. We all had a great time. At the end of the night, my girlfriend mentioned how well-mannered Frank was. She was mad that I suggested he was anything but a gentleman.

On another occasion, I attended a memorial service at a Masonic Temple for a popular union ally. The place was packed full of family, friends, labor folks, politicians and news media. Near the conclusion of the ceremony, the public were invited to say a few words. The business manager got up relating a conversation he had with the deceased. He unleashed a torrent of profanity. The crowd winced at his blasphemous language. He seemed unaware of the small children present and the sacrilegious nature of using such language in a temple. It didn't go over well.

100. Use Their Name Often

Do you forget people's names? You're not alone. One way to combat such a problem is to consciously use the person's name in initial conversations. There's a fundamental benefit that arises from doing so. The person will love that you remembered their name. It's like music to their ears.

101. Guard Your Reputation

Guard your reputation as a hawk guards it's young. Don't be clumsy when it comes to how people perceive you professionally. Give it due attention. Who's talking smack? Call the person on the carpet.

102. Maintain Relationships

Relationships grow over time, so make a conscious effort to keep in touch. The longer we know someone, the more significant the connection. Recognize opportunities to maintain healthy relationships. Nurture them along by recognizing important milestones such as birthdays, anniversaries, holidays and any other excuse to keep communication open. Be there for people not only when you are in need, but when others are lacking.

A very successful organizer, who is still rising through the ranks to prominence, seems to have a gift for remembering and maintaining good relationships with employers. Whenever the name of an employer is mentioned, he recognizes the name and can give a synopsis of the company. These relationships were first established through personal introductions and industry events. Holidays and milestones presented opportunities to reach out and reacquaint himself. Soon he knew the top players in the industry and more importantly, they knew him. Even after leaving the local organizing position to take on a national role, he trains and helps new organizers with the knowledge and relationships that were maintained.

103. Stick with Quality Organizing Materials

There are some great examples of well-designed, eye-catching quality organizing materials. They are a breath of fresh air. Still, some organizers are using outdated embarrassing, bland, cheap, crap. You know if you've used them. Hold out for quality next time. Redesign materials if needed. If there's funding for every politician who knocks at the hall door, there should be enough left over for decent organizing materials. Don't distribute anything that doesn't represent you, the local, or the union as top-notch.

Around 50 were coming into membership, though some of the workers expressed apprehension. We knew they were putting on a show to remain in good favor with the boss. Just in case, the local had a banner made welcoming the group. We prepared the paperwork in advance. Each person would get a color folder with union bug to take home. Inside were union pens, stickers, medical insurance brochures, Collective Bargaining Agreements, Bylaws and some organizing brochures. We wanted all their non-union buddies to contact us. The group arrived at the same time hanging out in the parking lot. There was some initial uneasiness, but they warmed up quick when they realized food was being served. The business manager welcomed everyone and brought them up to speed. Everyone completed the membership paperwork. There were no holdouts. We even took a group photo with the banner. We received dozens of calls in the weeks that followed from their friends who also wanted to join. No doubt the banner and pizzas helped, but the quality organizing materials looked fantastic!

104. Plan to Leave a Legacy

While working on the final section of my second book, The Green Career Ladder I took a vacation to the Grand Canyon and Yellowstone National Park with my then 11-year-old son. The park's beauty and grandeur amazed me, but what struck me most on this trip was the genius and foresight of men like Stephen Mather, John Muir, J. Horace McFarland and Robert Sterling Yard, whose efforts protected this land from development and led to the creation of the National Park Service.

With the proper plan in place, you too can leave a lasting legacy that will touch the lives of thousands, perhaps even millions of people throughout the world. As I've said elsewhere in this book and others, you're going to spend a good portion of your life in the workplace anyway, so why not use that time in a way that benefits society and improves the lives of future generations?

Think of your organizing career as a gift to yourself and your children – perhaps even to their children and beyond. How might this one choice lay the cornerstone for something even greater in coming years?

Now I hear many of you saying: "Hey, wait a minute – I'm just getting started and you want me to think about all this stuff now?" You may find it difficult to imagine. Whatever you may feel about your prospects today, it's important to realize that every choice you make, however small, will one day be appreciated.

Why think about legacy now?

Many people believe that a legacy is something you think about later in life after you've achieved some benchmark of success or in your final days just before you die. That's not how it works. Lasting legacies are built over the course of a lifetime, leveraging the gains you make as you go and encouraging you on to new heights. That's why the best time to think about your legacy is now.

Altruism is a noble and worthy goal but incorporating your long-term vision into your plan also makes it more likely that you'll enjoy success and prosperity throughout your career. Here's why:

- A legacy plan makes you more accountable for your results, so you're less likely to waste time. Knowing that you're mortal and that the clock is ticking can be an amazing motivation.

- Having a clear vision of exactly what you're trying to accomplish, which will make you less vulnerable to distraction and keep you focused on your goals.

- Key education and career choices will be easier for you than for most people. Tough decisions are easily put into perspective when you ask the question:" Which option will help me achieve my long-term goals most effectively?" If you have a clear goal for the future, everything else is more likely to fall into place.

- You'll lead a happier and more satisfying life even if you don't achieve all your goals. Scientific research into human happiness is a relatively new field, but recent studies suggest that people who regularly give to a charitable cause – by donating money or blood, for example – are as much as 43% more likely to say they are "very happy" about their lives no matter what income bracket they're in. If giving makes people happier, what career could be better than union organizing?

The entire labor movement is rooted in the value of long-term benefits, so success isn't just about us. Making the legacy you wish to leave behind a key part of your goals is more than just a good idea; it's essential if you want to maximize your influence and success.

105. Embrace Transparency

We need to be transparent in dealing with people and keep everyone informed of progress. Our message must be unified. If one organizer is saying one thing and another is saying something entirely different there are going to be repercussions. Technology makes it possible, even likely that contradictory messaging will be shared instantly. It's now more important than ever to be transparent in our dealings. Even presidential campaigns have been affected by mixed messaging and lack of transparency.

106. Build a Database of Candidates

Having an updated database of employers and workers would be a powerful tool. Imagine organizing a jurisdiction knowing exactly which nonunion employers were in the area and how much workers are being paid. Wouldn't it be nice to be able to send the workers information about opportunities offered by the union? If you became aware that a nonunion employer was about to go bankrupt, it would be nice to call the employees to inquire about their plans to find work and offer to help. Having a database of candidates is a good way to organize contacts.

List Workers

When contacted by workers, add them to the list. Record the contact's name, address, phone number, employer, experience level, and any other pertinent details. Were you contacted by phone? Did you meet the person at their workplace? What was the issue that seemed to be on the person's mind? Stay on top of changes to keep your list updated. Take advantage of opportunities to contact workers with information such as recent raises in the contract, new classes, or new benefits offered to members.

List Employers

For employers, add the name of the business, owners, or key individuals such as the chief executive officer; address; phone number; fax number; license; type of work specialty. Add the website address and other details. As more information comes in, add notes and record the date of your entry.

107. Scrounge for Resources

Keep an eye out for anything that can help you organize better. Things like union shirts, stickers, hats, and pins, can be used to entice members to volunteer. Maybe you want to improve the quality of your mailings. Hold out for the 24lb paper. Political campaigns are notorious for wasting huge amounts of full color printed materials, office supplies, individually wrapped snacks and sodas. After a race for mayor, a dumpster full of lawn signs were discarded. We collected the wireframes and used them for an organizing drive. Always keep an eye out for opportunities.

A very effective business representative gained a reputation going to various satellite offices on a mission for freebies. He would request things such as union buttons, pins, and koozies, anything he could share with members. If there was lip balm or toothbrushes given away at the retirement seminar, he would grab handfuls. The local had a passenger van, and he made quick use of it. Some people thought he just wanted to save wear and tear on his own tires, but it wasn't long before people realized he was organizing. Whenever we had an event where we relied on members to volunteer, he would show up with the most people. He could pack a city council meeting or hearing with members.

108. Guard Your Time

We are all given just twenty-four hours each day to accomplish the things we want to achieve. The only difference between those who succeed and those who don't is how wisely we use that time. It's easy to get distracted. We let our mind wander for a moment while online or doing menial tasks and the next thing we know an hour or two has gone by. We can't get that time back. It takes self-discipline to stay focused amongst all the distractions.

If we were to track our time spent during a typical work day, we would be able to identify opportunities for improvement. Careful use of time management skills can help increase our effectiveness. It's easy to get side-tracked by all the distractions and responsibilities that come along with the job. Phone calls need to be returned, meetings require our attendance, and employers are spread out all over the place. How is an organizer supposed to fit all these activities into a day?

The answer is planning. Planning starts by prioritizing the next day's activities. Take a few minutes at the end of each afternoon to plan the next workday. Then create a "To Do" list with urgent priorities on the top and less urgent priorities on the bottom. Include steps required to complete each task. Be flexible and allow plenty of time for each step. This is something that often gets overlooked. We need to consider possible distractions and roadblocks. Things like traffic and unforeseen last-minute assignments.

During the holidays, having dropped by the local's main office to drop off paperwork, I was commandeered to deliver gift baskets across town. It was the height of the Christmas season. Traffic was snarled in all directions. Last minute things will come up. It will sometimes make time management difficult. Add priorities to the list and take pleasure in checking them off as completed.

109. Don't Wait for Washington

Organize like always, regardless of who's in office. It's tempting to think a labor-friendly regime in the White House, Congress or Senate will make a huge difference, but it never really does. Nothing to watch here. Move on!

A monthly meeting of union organizers on the west coast helped alleviate the problem of organizers not communicating about similar targets. A week or so after the November elections, with a supposedly friendly administration preparing to take office, one organizer recommended taking a wait-and-see approach to evaluate the coming administration's policies. Promises were made to labor by politicians seeking office. "Card-check" would abolish the secret ballot. It would streamline the NLRB process finally giving unions an edge. Everyone knew labor wanted the proposed changes. How long would it take the new president to implement such measures? Some thought the changes would be made within a few weeks, other's months. A decade later, nothing's ever been done. They were empty promises by people who have been reelected regardless of their effectiveness. Card check was the flavor of the season, forgotten by labor and politicians alike. That is, until the next election four years later.

110. Provide Freebies Like T-Shirts, Hats, Stickers, etc.

Members want to show their union pride. Share union shirts, hats, stickers, pins and buttons with members in the hall, hardworking volunteers and their families. Some locals bogart these items, then wonder why they have such low turn-out at meetings and events. The sooner we get these items out of the office and into member's hands the better.

There was an apprentice skills competition taking place in Los Angeles. They needed graduates to judge the event. A coworker on the construction site we were working on asked if I would be interested in being a judge. It was a great experience. The level of expertise demonstrated by all competitors was amazing. Any employer would be lucky to have such professionals working for their company. As a token of appreciation, we were invited to a buffet dinner and given a custom union t-shirt. The next day I wore it on the job. Members were asking where I got it and could they get one. "The only way to get one of these is by volunteering," I said.

111. Practice the Gift of Gab

Union organizers are natural communicators. Some have taken the art of conversation to new levels. You'll know you've engaged in great conversation when you walk away feeling energized and can't wait to reconnect. We should all strive to improve by practicing the gift of gab. Conversations are where ideas and observations flow freely between interested parties. Like a game of catch, the ball needs to move back and forth between participants. That makes listening every bit as important as talking. When we first meet someone, we are curious to find out who they are, where they are from and what they do. We can discover what their values are as the conversation continues.

112. Volunteer in Your Community

We already know the value of volunteering in our unions, consider branching out to reach more people in the community. My guess is, you volunteer in a variety of capacities. If not, then find a cause and get busy. Doing so will prepare you to be useful when thrown into almost any situation.

There was a church that ran a homeless shelter out of a basement in Santa Monica, California. They ran a classified ad in the paper looking for volunteers. I envisioned myself chopping vegetables in the kitchen along with 10 to 15 volunteers under the direction of a chef. That was not the case. Instead, I was given a walk-through by a very busy caretaker who informed me there would be 45 people to feed at 6 am Sunday morning, so be ready. No one else responded to the ad.

Luckily, I had a history of community service for a variety of causes and knew how to hit-the-bricks running. The prep work was all done at home the evening before. If they saw the shotgun-shack I was living in at the time, they might have protested. The menu consisted of breakfast burritos, pancakes, oatmeal, cold cereals, fresh fruit, toast, milk, orange juice, and coffee. The residents really appreciated the effort. Restaurants donated day-old bagels and donuts, etc. Over the next 6 months or so, other volunteers showed up. Some were helpful and others seemed to get in the way. The volunteers who showed up with a good attitude and were willing to do just about anything proved to be the most helpful.

113. Take an Annual Vacation

Ever noticed how people who take time to travel just seem to live happier more interesting lives? You can too. Take an annual vacation. See new sights. Plan that once-in-a-lifetime trip. Change things up. Trade the timeshare in. Don't settle for the same old routine. We'll have more to talk about, more stories to share. Someone will mention a destination and we'll be able to tell them all about the place. Drink up the whole experience leaving nothing behind.

We all want to be around interesting people, that go after their dreams. They scrimp and save; somehow managing to afford the best destinations, guided hunting trips, cabins in the mountains, ski trips, and cruises. If we were their supervisor and canceled their vacation they would probably drag-up. Let's be more like that. We work hard. We deserve it.

A coworker was always talking about taking her kids on a Disney Cruise. For some reason, it got postponed from one year to the next. She could easily afford it. They lived in a new house and drove nice cars. The kids were getting older. Soon they'd be teenagers. That Fall, she became ill. We visited her in the hospital. She endured chemotherapy, lost her hair and miraculously began to get better. She stubbornly returned to work, though she could probably have remained on disability. On at least one occasion while dispatching members she put the mic on mute and vomited into a wastebasket. It was heartbreaking to see her so ill. We begged her to go home and take care of herself. She insisted she was alright, but it was obvious she wasn't ready to return to work yet.

Over the next few months, her health improved. We talked about the future a lot. The cancer had no effect in changing her outlook.

We encouraged her to finally take that Disney Cruise with the family. She shrugged the idea off. She just wanted things to be back to normal, to catch up on lost time.

The sound of the carbon steel casket sliding against the abrasive concrete vault of the mausoleum still gives me the chills. It's a reminder of how short life is. It's the sound of unfulfilled dreams. The best time to take young kids on vacation is right now. Take an annual vacation. Make it a habit.

114. Be Persistent

Persistence is often the key to success in any venture. Many top achievers had terrible setbacks along the way, before reaching critical mass and victory. It's almost as if life throws us a few stumbling blocks to test our fortitude. We must push forward through these setbacks and be persistent to win.

In December 2016, I volunteered along with dozens of union organizers to help organize workers at Baltimore Gas and Electric in Maryland. Being from sunny California, I had never experienced cold weather like that in my life. We conducted house calls and greeted workers at the gates. There were several previous election attempts that ended in defeat. This time, however, the workers voted 751 to 610 in favor of the union. Afterward, someone told me they had been trying to unionize the unit since the union was founded.

115. Have Email Checked Before Sending

Whether we are sending emails or texts or any other important correspondence, consider having the message proofread. Email is a fast, easy, and inexpensive way to communicate with candidates, prospects, and co-workers. It differs from traditional mail because it's less formal and more likely to get a quick response or multiple responses.

Email is more permanent than we might think. Unlike telephone calls, where we may feel a certain amount of privacy, with email, it's a whole different story. Some think because they erased an email, it can't be retrieved. Email can be retrieved, and it can be subpoenaed as part of a legal proceeding too. This goes for text messages as well. Email is a great way to communicate, but there are some dos and don'ts to consider:

- Do use a spell checker

- Do reread what is written

- Don't use all capital letters

- Don't use sarcasm

- Do ask for permission before sending attachments

- Don't leave the subject line blank

- Do use BCC or blind carbon copy when mass emailing

- Do respond to emails quickly

Two of us worked on a correspondence to be sent to nonunion workers in the area. We had it proofread by everyone in the office. In a meeting that followed the subject of the correspondence was brought up and the best time to send it was discussed. The group decided to shorten the message to keep it brief and to the point. The business manager wanted to see it before it was sent. He made a few improvements including adding his name instead of the organizers. When the message was finally sent, the phone started ringing and the calls were routed back to the organizers. The finished version was far more effective than the original.

116. Know Your Ideal Candidate

If you send a dozen candidates to be placed into the apprenticeship, and they all get turned-away, you're not doing anyone any good. Find out specifically, what your union's requirements are for membership. Does an apprentice need a GED or high school diploma? How many hours' experience to become a journeyman? Is there a written test? Is there a hands-on equivalent of the test? Know your ideal candidate.

117. Write a Press Release

A well-written press release can bring much-needed media attention. Say we want to promote the union's open house, or alert the public to attend a protest rally, all that is needed are a few basic details. Most press releases start with "FOR IMMEDIATE RELEASE" all caps, followed by a catchy headline in bold letters and answer the questions; who, what, when, where, and why. It should include contact information and end with three hashtags ### near the bottom of the page. Look for sample press releases online or hire a service to make and distribute one for you.

118. Smile When Making Phone Calls

Somehow, we humans can tell when the person on the other side of the phone is smiling. It might be the tonality or the facial expression, either way, we can perceive the presence of a smile. A study by the University of Portsmouth, England found not only can we tell if a person is smiling, but what type of smile. It works for recorded messages as well. Next time you make a call smile. Let the other person know you are happy to be speaking with them.

119. Study Worker Ideology

People's expectations of what a job is have changed dramatically over the years. What may have motivated someone in the 1990's, might drive another away today. People in different industries sometimes see work differently. Artists in the Visual Effects industry for example, often don't see themselves as "workers" in the classic sense. They don't like the idea of comparing what they do to someone working in a factory. Become familiar with people's beliefs, goals, and expectations. Study worker ideology, especially in the industries we work in. Don't ignore it. Study it.

120. Hold Your Calls

One of the best ways to show respect for people is to hold our calls and turn off our cell phones. Once we start implementing this policy people seem to reciprocate. Give people the gift of undivided attention. Practice active listening and avoid any distractions that might interrupt the conversation.

121. Give Them an Out

Take the pressure off people so they can come to their own conclusion. Individuals will be more open to meeting with us if they know we aren't pushing anything on them. It's perfectly normal for a person to want to take a few days to consider a decision affecting their future.122.

122. Visualize a Winning Outcome

If we can see a win in our mind it will be easier to bring to fruition. Visualize a winning outcome. How will you feel? What will you say? How will you celebrate? What still needs to be done?

123. When You Aren't Sure, Get Back to Them

None of us has all the answers, but we probably know who to ask. When we can't answer a question or aren't certain, it's ok. The best policy is to let the person know and make every effort to find out and get back to them.

124. Study Body Language

Become familiar with non-verbal cues. They tend to give away more information than most people are aware of. Study body language to become a better communicator. Incorporate the use of non-verbal communication to project confidence.

125. Know Your Competition

First, know you have competition. Some are in denial of the fact. There are outside sources; unions, companies, associations, recruiting services, all trying to eat your lunch. How do they add up? What things are they likely to say? What is their usual reaction? How can you compete? Look for answers, know your competition.

126. Practice Presentation Skills

Most presenters don't practice enough, and it shows. It isn't enough to put a PowerPoint together and read through it twice. We need to review the information until we know it cold, and include as many techniques to keep the audience engaged. We should always have a backup plan in case the microphone, projector or computer stops working. Beware of the no-it-all's that take pleasure in tripping presenters up.

Give a gift to your audience.

A great speech is like a well-chosen present from someone we admire. We all want our presentations to have an impact. We want our speeches to be remembered and appreciated to make a difference in the lives of those we speak to. The best speeches leave lasting impressions. To really grab their attention, we need to choose topics of interest specifically to those in the audience. What interests do we share? What common needs do we have? What would benefit the audience and keep their attention?

Look for clues; they're there just waiting to be discovered. In some groups, it's more obvious than others. They may have a theme or an interest that attracts members. It might be in the name itself.

People leave clues for active listeners. When meeting someone new, it's a good practice to ask questions and then allow the individual to answer without interruption. Most of us love to talk about ourselves. Allow people the courtesy of your full and undivided attention. Of course, there are some who are shy and keep things close to the vest. If this is the case listen to see how they answer to see if you can pick up additional clues as to their interests.

You may wonder does the other person have pets, like cars, where are they from, what kind of place do they call home? Do they have a favorite food? Do they cook? Make a mental list.

Now consider adding these interests in your next speech. Create content by carefully choosing the right ingredients like a master chef would in a fine restaurant. It should satisfy the individual's needs or wants and pull the person's attention in.

Right from the start, the title should tell the audience; listen up! This is something that will interest you. Don't hide the intent or subject. Let it show and entertain. Motivate the audience to act. Share a little personal information about who you are and how the subject relates to you. Connect with the audience by adding visuals or gestures to strengthen the message. Inject your own enthusiasm into the subject which will be appreciated and reciprocated. Wrap it up with just the right voice inflection and eye contact. Your audience will have as much fun receiving your gift as you will have delivering it.

127. Study Maslow's Hierarchy of Needs

Psychologist Abraham Maslow came up with a brilliant theory to explain human needs. The five motivations are psychological, safety, love, esteem, and self-actualization. By familiarizing ourselves with these five human needs and the importance of their order, we can better understand what motivates individuals to do what they do.

128. Refocus the Conversation

One question that always comes up when speaking to potential members is, "will I be out of work if we go union?" The best response might be a question, "why would you be out of work?" Listen carefully for clues to what the concern is. Often a union buster or a manager will tell workers if they go union the company will leave town or some other ridiculous story. Sometimes a coworker will have a grudge against unions and spread misinformation. If you ask where they heard it, you might find it was a cousin of a guy not familiar with your union. Asking a few questions refocuses the conversation to the responsibility of the worker. Use the opportunity to explain what a union is and how it can benefit the workers.

129. Use Inclusive Words "We" and "Us"

Help people feel more comfortable by using inclusive words such as "we" and "us." Be welcoming and the community will respond accordingly.

130. Close the Door to Your Office

Want to get pulled into every situation, every conversation that arises in the office? Want to be consulted about all the trivialities of the modern workplace? Would you like members to dump their troubles on your plate? How about being a go-between when coworkers gossip? Would you like your personal conversations to become public knowledge? Of course not. Here's a tip to dramatically increase productivity and decrease interruptions. Adopt a closed-door policy. Obviously, this won't work if you occupy a cubical. A closed-door policy doesn't mean you aren't available if a member has a problem. It doesn't mean you don't accept phone calls. It's a simple reminder to others that you value your time and concentration. There's a phrase used on construction sites, "we set our own conditions." The contract is the minimum standard. The workers are constantly adding niceties. Here's a chance to up your own conditions in the office.

131. Address Common Objections

Management will always ask for a second chance. They will attempt to paint the union as "outsiders" or a third party. They intentionally confuse workers with misinformation about dues, fines, and fees. The fear of increased costs to the individual is going to come up.

You can't avoid it. Get it out in the open and address workers concerns before management has an opportunity. Other topics likely to come up when management holds captive audience meetings are; company closings, union salaries, strikes, negotiations starting from scratch, company never signing a contract, loss of benefits, lazy workers, etc.

132. Learn to Enjoy Mondays

What is it with Mondays? Some people curse the day, while others enjoy it. Is it because we are exhausted from so much activity over the weekend? Is it the anxiety of showing up for work? Could it be because our sleep patterns are off? What makes Monday so intolerable? Whatever the reason, we need to take it seriously. Statistically, the highest number of suicides happen on Sunday evening. At least we've passed that hurdle.

We'll enjoy Monday's if we include more fun activities and don't overload our schedules. Try rewarding yourself with delicious food. Schedule some personal time to decompress. Listen to uplifting recordings or your favorite music. Avoid following the news which seems to focus on everything negative. Learning to enjoy Mondays is a sign of maturity. Once Monday is completed we can focus on Tuesday, which studies show is our most productive day.

133. Look Beyond Friction

Whenever there's a campaign or staff working intensely for weeks on end, there's going to be friction. There may be differences of opinion on how to proceed or individuals who can't seem to get along. Sometimes it's petty jealousy, other times it's more than that. The long hours and time away from home wear people down. Some of us get caught up in the squabble wanting a resolution to the matter. Times like these, force us to look beyond the friction, continuing the work needed to succeed. The alternative is to get mired in the weeds.

134. Don't Panic

Management held a captive audience meeting and some workers may have been spooked. No need to worry. You met with the workers in advance and warned them this would happen. Panicking sometimes causes organizers to be reactionary and that's not a position of power in an organizing campaign. It's better when we control the message and management reacts. Keep cool when hit with surprises and don't panic.

135. Prioritize Your To-Do List

If we were to track our time spent during a typical work day, would we be able to identify opportunities for improvement? The answer is probably, "Yes." Careful use of time management skills can help us increase our effectiveness. It's easy to get sidetracked by all the distractions and responsibilities that come along with a job. Phone calls need to be returned, meetings require our attendance, and workers are spread out all over the jurisdiction. How is an organizer supposed to fit all these activities into a day?

The answer is planning. Planning starts by prioritizing the next day's activities. Take a few minutes at the end of each afternoon to plan your next workday. Then create a "To Do" list with urgent priorities on the top and less urgent priorities on the bottom. Include steps required to complete the task. Be flexible and give yourself plenty of time for each step.

136. Familiarize Yourself with Union-Busting Videos

"Know your enemy." – Sun Tzu, The Art of War

There are tons of examples online of videos companies use to discourage employees from organizing. We need to familiarize ourselves with the messaging union-busters are using, to thwart their efforts. Employers often begin indoctrination of workers right after hiring.

137. Prepare for Negotiations

From the day of the election win, efforts should be focused on achieving a fair and equitable written contract for the workers. Survey the workers in the bargaining group to find out what issues are most important to them. Assemble a bargaining committee that is representative of all departments and workers. Schedule regular meetings to inform the members of progress.

138. Empower Volunteer Organizers

"The best way to find out if you can trust somebody is to trust them." - Earnest Hemingway

Empower volunteer organizers to help. The sooner we delegate, the easier our jobs will be. Organizer burnout is a problem. Union members are more than happy to assist with organizing if given the opportunity and clear instructions.

What duties will be delegated? We can start out slowly by simply including volunteers in picketing or leafleting. Later as we become more familiar with their abilities, we may wish to include them in salting or phone banking.

139. Thank Volunteers Publicly

Whenever members volunteer, take a group photo. It will help mark the occasion as well as help you to remember exactly who showed up to help. Then find some way to reward all the volunteers for their efforts. Few people ever volunteer just once. In fact, it may seem that you lean on the same individuals repeatedly. It's important to recognize their efforts publicly. You might consider presenting volunteers with a certificate of appreciation at the next union meeting or posting a photo with a note of thanks in the union hall or on the website. Reward volunteers with free t-shirts, hats, stickers, and buttons. They've given you their time. It's the one thing they can never get back. Show appreciation for their efforts and do it publicly.

140. Invite Members to Speak to VOC

Bring current members to speak with potential members. They can answer worker's questions and have similar experience in the field. Make sure you get someone enthusiastic who can handle tough questions.

We were organizing a group of technicians up north. There was a similar group down south that went union years earlier. Both groups worked for the same company. I requested one of the union members participate in a conference call with the nonunion workers and he enthusiastically agreed. We met at the local union's office sitting around a conference table with the cellphone in the center. Even set to high volume, the group had to be quiet to hear. There was cross-talk and some interruptions but overall, the conference call was a success. The nonunion workers were concerned about implementation of a point system they were working under. The union worker knew all about the point system, having worked under it for years, but informed the group the union successfully negotiated that out of the contract a few years back. They were amazed. After answering all their questions, the member provided his personal cell phone number in case anyone wanted to call at another time. It worked beyond our expectations.

141. Familiarize Yourself with "Right to Work" Laws

Become knowledgeable with Right-to-Work laws and how they hurt unions and worker's wages. Research on both sides of the issue is biased and unreliable. It's almost impossible to compare one state's economy with another given all the variables. One thing is clear, however, when dues money is decreased there's less money for union organizing and that hurts membership growth. At the time of this writing, there are twenty-six states with Right to Work laws in place. It's obvious that if something isn't done, soon the entire nation will adopt such laws and labor's influence will be further diminished.

142. Start a Speakers Bureau

A speaker's bureau is nothing more than a list of potential speakers qualified to speak on a given topic. There's a need for knowledgeable speakers in the Labor movement. Too often conference facilitators rely on the same people year after year. Have you noticed lawyers or academics with little or no experience organizing being asked to address organizers? What's the point? It's boring! Who wants to endure another rehashed speech with information you can't use? Instead, why not start a Speaker's Bureau?

Identify members and retirees who could speak on a variety of Labor related topics such as organizing, right to work, women's issues, safety, politics, etc. Invite them to be speakers at events. Promote the group to expand labor's influence.

143. Ask for Recommendations

You brought in a new member doubling their pay and now they are vested in the pension and are covered by the medical plan. Ask the member for a recommendation. Nothing too fancy. It can be scribbled on a notepad. Just make sure you have the member's permission to use it for recruiting new members. Share it with nonunion workers and prospective members. People need an example of someone who has succeeded. It helps them visualize themselves in a better situation.

144. Ask Workers to Pen Exit Letters to Management

When you get someone to leave a nonunion dead-end job for a good paying union career, ask the person to pen an exit letter to their last employer. Workers know exactly why they left their last job, offer them an opportunity to tell management. Sometimes management is still in the dark. A letter explaining why the company lost a valued employee might make them more careful in the future.

145. Follow Up with a Letter and Business Card

You've made initial contact with potential candidates for the union, but they don't always follow through as expected. There's a fool-proof system to stay in touch until they sign up. One way to do this is with follow-up mailings. It may seem like overkill at first, following up a phone call with a letter and business card sent via the mail, but it's not. By initiating a follow-up, you will stay in better touch with potential candidates and increase the number of workers who ultimately become members.

146. Add a Humorous Cartoon

There are some great labor cartoonists that really know how to tackle the issues. For a small fee, you can license their work and reuse it on websites, pamphlets, handbills, and flyers.

147. Be Resilient

"It is not the strongest of the species that survives, not the most intelligent, but the one most responsive to change." - Charles Darwin

Change isn't the only challenge you'll face in your career – you're also going to experience some setbacks and disappointments. You might lose a tough campaign, get passed over for a promotion you feel you deserve, be discriminated against in some way, experience a health-related problem, or care for a loved one who gets sick. You might get divorced and be ordered to pay child support. These are common challenges, but they can all be overcome.

The same strategies that can help you adapt to rapid change also apply to setbacks. The secret to beating it is to look for opportunities. Learn to shake things off and start over.

In 1994 I lived in Tarzana, which is only a few miles from Northridge, California. At 4:30 am on January 17 of that year, I was one of the thousands of people in Greater Los Angeles to be hit by what is now known as the "Northridge Earthquake," which weighed in at 6.7 on the Richter magnitude scale. To put that in perspective, you'd need about 16.2 megatons of dynamite to cause the same amount of damage, and the most powerful magnitude that can be measured reliably is 6.8. It was only slightly weaker, as these things go than the San Francisco Bay Area earthquake of 1989. It was a whopper!

I was already awake when the earthquake struck. I had just turned my alarm off and was standing in my bedroom thinking:" I'm so exhausted. How am I going to get up?" Then BOOM! That earthquake hit and finding the motivation to go to work was suddenly the least of my problems. I was literally thrown up into the air, and my first thought was that a nuclear bomb had hit the area.

I had a beautiful 27-gallon saltwater fish tank in my living room. It was hurled all the way across the room and smashed. I couldn't save any of the fish by putting them into fresh water. The power was knocked out. All the glass inside my condo was broken. The door to my bedroom was jammed shut. It was just unbelievable.

My neighbors ran downstairs to make sure I was okay, saying: "Thank God we've all got insurance!" But that only made things worse for me: I had just canceled my insurance policy. Two weeks before I had briefly been laid off for a week or two, and when that bill came I panicked. I remember thinking to myself: "There hasn't been an earthquake here in 30 years. What am I paying this thing for?" So, I checked the little box to cancel the policy.

I took a serious beating that year. I lost more than $50,000 from the quake itself, and it got worse because I went into damage control mode right afterward. I started patching walls, replacing windows, and doing all kinds of other construction work myself. In six to eight weeks I had the whole place looking great – until the inspectors came. They found a crack in the slab from my condo all the way across a bunch of other units, so they condemned the whole building. We all had to move out. Construction crews came in, jack hammered all the flooring I had installed and tore out all the drywall that I had just painted and patched.

The homeowner's association had earthquake insurance even though I didn't, and that covered the cost of rebuilding the whole unit. But the whole time I had to pay the mortgage and rent a place to stay. For a long time, I wasn't sure if I was going to lose my unit to foreclosure. On top of that, I still had to go to work every day and deal with all the regular problems we all have.

It was really tempting to just give up, but I kept working because I didn't want to damage my credit. I knew things were going to get better. My family and friends helped me a lot. I had a fantastic job. I just kept going to work every day and I managed to get through it. I found the opportunities, the silver lining, and the whole time I was thinking to myself: "Hey, when this thing is done, I'm going to be living in a brand-new place."

Today I wish I had bought ten other condos at the time. After the earthquake, the owners couldn't sell them, and the price went down to $27,000 each for a time. Meanwhile, my condo was rebuilt, and it was better than before. They shear-walled it and brought it up to code so that it was as strong as a bomb shelter.

The builder let me go in during construction to add extra insulation and run new phone lines in places where I didn't have any before. I added more electrical outlets and custom features, making it more the way I wanted it. I knew the whole time that it was going to increase in value and be a better place, and it was. Just a few years later, the people who had just given up and walked away were kicking themselves.

Disaster experiences like this may happen to you, and there's nothing you can do to prevent them. But when and if they do, look hard to find opportunities in disguise. You may find, as I did, that the future is much brighter on the other side.

148. Create a Young Workers Group

According to the Bureau of Labor Statistics in 2018 more than seventy-five percent of new union members were under the age of thirty-four. Many local unions have helped create groups to help empower and connect young workers. Such groups get together sharing information for mutual support.

147. Avoid Burning Bridges

Avoid alienating people and burning bridges. It's amazing how often we run into the same people during a career. One day we're on top of the world, the next we're signing the out-of-work book.

Ten Mistakes Union Organizers Make

Year after year union organizers make mistakes that cause their careers to end abruptly. Others lose attitude and the slow progression of negativity takes its toll over time. Some of the best organizers burn-out from the workload and return to the tools taking their organizing skills and training with them. How can we avoid making these tragic mistakes and assure we will have a successful career as a union organizer? Read this list of ten mistakes union organizers need to avoid and check to see if you're making these career mistakes.

1. Not Returning Phone Calls – Candidates, members, and contractors all expect to have phone calls returned in a timely manner. Some organizers forget this fact at their own expense. If you fail to return calls, expect to receive a call from your Supervisor or Business Manager. Nothing says, "I don't care" like an unreturned phone call. Consider scheduling a time each day for returning calls and stick to it.

2. Hanging Around the Office – Get out in the field and contact workers. Don't let distractions in the office; phone calls, paperwork, member's problems, etc. steal time from organizing duties. Get out there and make a difference.

3. Failure to Complete Written Reports – If requested to turn-in daily logs or other written reports make these a priority. This is an opportunity to inform the supervisor of your actions. Don't assume they know what you are doing. Schedule time each day to

complete paperwork and turn it in like clockwork. Don't wait to be told.

4. Bad-Mouthing Your Boss or Co-workers – It may take a year or so but eventually this leads to a bad attitude and once you lose attitude there's no getting it back. It "will" get back to them. If you make a habit of speaking ill of people, soon everyone will wonder what you've said about them when they weren't around. Successful people always have something positive to say or they just stay silent.

5. Waiting to be Told What to Do – Most organizers are self-starters. If we haven't been given an assignment, we make one. Pick a project you're interested in and throw all your energy into it. If it's interesting to you, you'll be that much more effective and more likely to make a difference. Most organizers are given a brief tour of their jurisdiction and a few guidelines to start and then turned loose. So, don't feel like you're alone.

6. Avoiding Workers Who Lack Experience – You may be the only representative of the union the worker ever contacts. It's important that you do everything you can to help a worker; that means every worker. It might be to find work, provide information or just to listen, but remember, "organizing is a service industry".

7. Selling the Union – If we're "selling the union", we're probably not "listening." Avoid doing all the talking. Remember, we're not selling used cars. The best union organizers learn to "listen". By listening we'll find out what the "issue" is so we can better serve the client.

8. Not Following-Up with Contacts – When we receive a phone call or meet with a client that's just the start. We need to be sure that we're staying in touch with people to be successful. Consider mailing a follow-up letter to the individual and include a business card. Thank clients for their time and encourage them to stay in touch.

9. Failing to Orientate New Members – New members have a lot of questions and by helping to answer these questions we can help

the person assimilate into the union. Does the union offer a new member orientation class or a mentoring program? We need to pair up new members with volunteers who are familiar with the union's culture? Perhaps we could invite the new member to join the organizing committee? Find some way to help each new member fit in and take ownership of their union.

10. Burning Out – The long hours required to organize can take a toll on a person. The hours and days spent away from home and family can cause stress in a marriage. Find a way to balance work and family. Take time-off, eat right and schedule time for exercise.

The turn-over rate of union organizers is tragic for the labor movement. There are no signs that anything will be done to solve the problem anytime soon. The best way to ensure success as an organizer is to avoid making these ten common mistakes so you can continue to help the union expand in membership and influence.

150. Know Your Role

In large organizing campaigns, there may be several organizers tasked with different responsibilities. Know your role and what is expected of you as a member of the team. Each person's contribution is important to the outcome. Problems start when organizers overstep their boundary. Only one person should run the campaign. That individual makes all final decisions about strategy and tactics.

151. Communicate with Your Supervisor

Find out your supervisor's preferred method of communicating and use it. Check-in to leave lines of communication open. Respond quickly and accurately to all requests.

152. Quit Complaining

We need to check ourselves, now and then, to make sure we're not falling into bad habits. When we're complaining, we aren't showing enough gratitude. That negativity can be contagious. Complainers are difficult to be around. They suck the energy out of a room and can be bad for morale. If we take responsibility for our thoughts, and redirect the energy toward solutions, those around us will appreciate it. We'll feel more energized.

153. Identify Roadblocks

Any endeavor worth pursuing will experience setbacks. If the union organizing process was easy, they wouldn't need organizers like us. The trick is to identify potential roadblocks to organizing and implement a strategy for success. It requires anticipation of management's activities and tactics. We need to constantly ask ourselves, "what will they do next?"

154. Identify Worker's Pain

When communicating with workers we need to listen for clues. What are the issues causing anxiety or discomfort? How are they coping with their situation? Look for reactions to identify the main issue.

155. Show Up Early

Make a habit of arriving early to appointments. Be mindful of other's time. When we show up early we ensure minor annoyances such as a late train, flat-tire or traffic don't ruin our day. We keep things in perspective by planning ahead. There's no fear of being called out for being late. We've left that for some other individual.

156. Take BIG Risks

Union organizing is not for the faint of heart. You are the face of the union. Take the message of solidarity and economic justice out to the workers. Go to the highest floor or the lowest basement. Leave the people that you meet in awe of your courage. Answer all their questions, no matter how basic. When you don't know an answer, admit it, but find someone who does and follow up. If you are asked to leave, leave, but come back the next day and the day after that.

I spent nearly a week undercover at the 1,000,000 square-foot Ronald Reagan UCLA Medical Center. It felt a little like working for the CIA. The project was under construction, behind schedule, and way over budget. I was photographing and documenting potential code violations by a nonunion contractor. Mornings I arrived like everyone else, lunch and thermos in hand, hardhat, boots, and reflective vest. I commandeered a rolling cart and moved methodically from room to room. There wasn't anywhere on the project I didn't go. Workers loaned me ladders, work lights, and cords. A buddy of mine who was a building inspector joined me on his day-off to uncover additional potential violations. He cited specific sections of the code for me to use when presenting my findings. At first, it was hair-raising being on the same jobsite where I had picketed the gate only days earlier. Didn't anyone recognize me? Apparently not, because I joked and conversed alongside many of the workers, including supervision. If you extend a tape measure on a construction site, most people think you belong there. The exercise made me realize how truly susceptible employers are to a creative union organizing campaign.

157. Take Your Work Home

Some of the best union organizers have admitted recruiting candidates in grocery lines, at church, and at family functions. Take your work home and always be organizing. Like a dedicated nurse at the scene of a car accident. Put your skills to work on and off the clock.

158. Acknowledge Fear and Self-Doubt

There will be times when we are given what may seem like impossible tasks. We might have concerns about our strengths and abilities. Acknowledge fear and self-doubt, but act anyway. Action trumps fear.

159. Don't Be a Victim

Being a victim takes energy, lots of energy. Energy that would probably be better utilized in other pursuits. Being a victim is contagious, it's hereditary, and has the power to steal your friendships and your happiness. Being labeled a victim is like being labeled, "a jerk." It's doesn't have to be permanent. Make the decision. Don't be a victim.

160. See the Big Picture

Sometimes we get so focused on the task at hand that the bigger picture gets forgotten. It's not only about winning elections and securing the first contract. The labor movement is about lifting people out of the depths of economic ruin and improving their status. It's also about engaging workers to take an active part in their future.

There have been times when a win could've easily been achieved, but because the company was in such poor shape, the correct decision was to disengage. It's never easy to walk away from what would have been a victory. No union can fix a company that has adopted disastrous business practices. See the big picture and look for ways to improve worker's lives.

161. Avoid Being Bourgeoisie

Don't act superior to the workers being organized. See the situation from their perspective. Let's always be lifting workers up despite their situations. Worker loyalty to their employer keeps some to remain in miserable positions where they are abused, underpaid and underappreciated. Let's not add to their heartache.

162. Keep Good Records

This is where some organizers run into trouble. If we're fine in-the-field, but back at the office the expenses or activity reports don't get completed, eventually we run afoul of the boss. It reflects negatively on the local union. Schedule time to keep good records and the job will be a whole lot easier.

163. Be the Go-To Person

Every jurisdiction has a go-to person. It's the individual everyone relies on for answers. It's not determined by authority, but by knowledge. The go-to person is a role model and mentor. Accessibility is a key determinate.

164. Know Their Motivations

What drives a person to choose the industry you work in? What circumstances on the job result in workers reaching out to the union for help? Who could you talk with to get an insider's view? Put the book down and set up a meeting. Quick!

165. Believe in People

Union organizing requires a certain amount of faith. Regardless of any doubts, we might have, we need to believe in people, if we're going to convince them to organize their workplace. We must pass the baton; confident others will rise to the occasion and follow instructions. It's too easy to write workers off as not having enough character, abilities, and ambition. Perhaps it's all the sob stories we're bombarded with every day on the news. Put all that aside and believe in people.

166. Avoid Self-Medicating

There's a lot to be said about being stone-cold-sober, especially when so many in society are self-medicating. No one requires us to partake in self-medicating. Leave peer-pressure in the past. There are compelling reasons for self-control. Alcohol and drugs have ended many organizer's careers. Campaigns have been compromised, families destroyed, and freedoms lost. To survive a social situation, like an organizing conference or an apprenticeship graduation dinner try ordering a nonalcoholic beer or a tonic water.

If anxiety gets too intense seek help or attend AA meetings. The point is, you are not alone.

Find alternative ways to cope with stress and anxiety. Indulge in a hobby or activity. I'm an "emotional eater." When I'm exhausted or had a rough day, I bust-out a thick spoon and a gallon of ice cream. Sure, I regret it later, but the hangovers nothing compared to a fifth of Scotch.

167. Conduct a Tour of the Union Training Facility

Some union training facilities are so spectacular, they're used to host industry events, attracting new members and employers. If your union's training facility is impressive, conduct tours and invite interested workers and employers to see it for themselves. Don't just give the person the address and hope someone at the facility gives the tour. Meet the individual at an agreed upon time and conduct the tour yourself. Be sure to get permission in advance in case there's an event taking place.

168. Share a Relevant Article

Find a news article on a subject of interest to a worker and share it. The key to a good relationship is communication. To be effective at union organizing, we need to make initial contact, listen to what the worker has to say and stay in contact. This way when the person needs our expertise, we will be better able to serve them. Take the time to understand the issue and craft a message to meet the needs of the individual. Let's say a worker's main concern is healthcare. The person has expressed reservations about not having medical and dental coverage. Find an article on the subject and send it to them. Attach a note with your business card, "saw this article and thought of your situation." Wait a few days and follow up with a phone call to see if the person is ready to make a move. Either way, you are staying in touch and leaving communication lines open.

169. Remember Birthdays

Would you like to be remembered as thoughtful? Remember people's birthday. It's an important date for us. Every year, my dentist sends me a postcard for my birthday. I may have to remind my wife and best friends, but not my dentist. Dentists do this for a reason. It works! It's a nice gesture, and what does it cost? Almost nothing. For a moment we remember them in a positive way. It's as if they never stabbed that needle in our gums or drilled a nerve during a root canal. If it can work for a torture chamber like a dentist office, it can work for you. I had a dentist pull four wisdom teeth out in a single sitting. He retired a week later. It's a wonder we trust dentists at all. It's gotta be the birthday cards…

170. Recruit the Best Candidates

Gain a reputation as the person that recruits the best candidates to represent the union. Look for passionate individuals who meet all the requirements of employment. Pay attention to every detail so application paperwork is complete before turning it in. Recruit quality over quantity. If the work picture slows down, employers will keep the most productive workers busy.

171. Review Priorities

Plans change over time. Benchmarks are achieved. Sometimes teams are shaken-up. A good practice is to stop on occasion to review priorities. Most businesses report earnings on a quarterly basis. This is a reasonable length of time. Ninety-days should be enough to see if things are heading in the right direction.

172. Practice Good Table Manners

Good table manners are essential. Union organizers should be mindful of time-tested, established rules for dining. No one's going to ding you for using the wrong fork but talking with a mouth full of food or being rude to servers is unacceptable. There are other objectionable behaviors such as cell phones ringing, blowing one's nose, picking one's teeth or slurping food. Good manners represent us well and keep us from offending others.

173. Drive an American Car

Hands down we Americans make the best cars. There I said it. The big American automobile, everyone in the world aspires to drive one. I know, I know, it's a sensitive subject. This one may be controversial. If you're from Canada or one of the states that have a foreign car company using union labor my apologies. What message does it send our members when we drive a foreign car? Sure, the lines have been blurred between what is foreign and what is domestic. The parts come from here, they are assembled there, whatever. If you have to go into an explanation, it's unclear. Drive an American car; problem solved.

174. Be a Responsible Consumer

Anyone who has ever spent a bitter cold morning on a picket line, even if only in support of another union, knows how disheartening it feels to have someone cross the line. Whether a coworker or a customer it's an act of violence. Our duty as union organizers is to lift worker's up, not suck the life out of them. Show solidarity to workers. Don't cross picket lines, sanctioned or not! Don't advise others to cross picket lines.

Avoid shopping at places where owners or management are rabidly opposed to worker's joining unions. Make a conscious effort to stay at union hotels and resorts. Tip workers generously.

175. Include Rank and File

It's amazing how many labor-related, political and community events union organizers attend each year. While many of these activities become routine to us, rank-and-file members would find them informative, even educational. How many ribbon-cutting ceremonies, awards dinners, political luncheons, and industry meetings are too many? Our waistlines might leave clues. Unions might be better served if instead of relying on paid staff to attend such events, rank-and-file members were included, freeing up union resources to focus on organizing. An argument against including rank-and-file members might be a concern about empowering people to run against the current administration. It's the same reason some leaders fail to properly promote union meetings in hope of low turnout.

176. Educate and Inform

Take time to educate and inform workers of their rights.

3 Diabolical Lies Told to Workers

The following are lies used to fool workers. They are so pervasive and repeated so often by business interests and politicians that many people have accepted them as facts. Knowledge is the best defense. Become familiar with these falsehoods to avoid becoming a victim and counter their attacks.

1. Trickle-down economics – The lie goes like this; the rich get richer, and it's a good thing for the middle-class and poor because the spending leads to more and better opportunities through job creation. They argue that a rising tide floats all boats, but they're the only ones who can afford one. Meanwhile, you drown in debt.

2. What's good for Wall Street is good for Main Street – If this lie seems similar to trickledown economics you're partly right. The lie goes like this; rich investors should not pay taxes on capital gains because that money is the grease that keeps the economy going. After all, you might discourage the rich from participating in the market and the middle-class and poor will suffer through loss of job opportunities.

As we saw with the seven-hundred-billion-dollar bailout of Wall Street in 2008, wealthy CEO's and millionaire investors got the government to save their corporations when they mismanaged them. The argument then became the government can't let us fail or everyone will be dragged down with us. Of course, it is the poor and middle-class that got stuck holding the bag when CEO's of major corporations fell asleep at the wheel.

3. Free trade is good for American workers – The lie goes like this; the benefit of being able to purchase less expensive imported goods will offset any pain caused by loss of jobs at home. Ask yourself; is it good when jobs get shipped overseas? Is it true that Americans won't do the work? Or is it more likely that they won't do the work for the low wages being offered? Is it really a benefit to ship products halfway around the globe when they can be made here at home?

Lies such as these are an insult to our intelligence. If not countered and countered vigorously they somehow become accepted as fact by the general public.

Labor needs advocates who will counter such falsehoods. Union organizers are uniquely suited for the job. Our ability to reach out and persuade workers gives us an edge. Personal contact with workers at their place of employment gives organizers credibility.

177. Know Group Dynamics

Every group has certain personalities. Learn to identify them.

Dynamics of an Organizing Group

Over the course of many years, it's become clear almost every organizing group contains similar personalities. These individuals create a seamless web easily recognizable to veteran organizers. Knowing these variables exist and recognizing their contribution to the whole will help in planning communications and scheduling.

The Leader

A leader is a person who sees the big picture. Things aren't right and if we all come together as a team we can make a difference. This is your key supporter for now, but beware, somewhere down the line this person may do a complete 180-degree turn. He or she has excellent work skills and has earned the respect of the group.

This person may resemble a manager or have experience being a manager in the past and is likely trusted with an employee list or knows where to get it. The leader may refer to other employees as "my guys" or similar reference. The leader may have already done some research and be in a rush to file. Your job is to slow the person down and gather the necessary information for a solid win.

The Quiet One

The quiet one is a strong silent type. He or she is a good listener, constantly looking for discrepancies in your message. Be aware of this. Do your homework and make certain you don't make any promises. You might be tempted to write this person off as unsupportive, but this individual may become your strongest ally over time. The quiet one will have questions. These can be answered now or if still unsatisfied, after when the group disperses. Be ready for a question about dues.

The Loudmouth

The loudmouth needs to be heard and tends to repeat the same issues. They initiate dialogue in meetings which can be to the groups' benefit. This person has already appointed themselves spokesperson during company meetings but was probably ignored by management. The loudmouth may ask a lot of questions, even answering them, and increase in volume if interrupted. This can seem disruptive at times, especially when trying to schedule brief meetings. Loudmouths often do initial research or have relatives involved in a union; wants to move quickly, wants reassurance of timely implementation. The loudmouth might not have the best work skills.

The Unconvinced

The unconvinced has concerns about change. This person wants to hear what the group thinks; about the need for a union and wants to do a cost versus benefits analysis. There are many possible reasons for such concerns. These will become apparent as questions are asked and answered.

The Non-Committal

The non-committal figures, "What's the rush?" This person agrees there is a need for a union but is not yet ready to sign a card. "You go first," is the attitude of the non-committal.

The Short Timer

The short timer is close to leaving the company. This can be an employee near retirement age or someone who has already found another job and given notice and therefore will not be affected by union membership.

The Newbie

The newbie may be a new hire or less experienced than other workers. The newbie has not been around long enough to know how the workplace has changed, and not yet earned the respect of the other workers. Seasoned workers may hesitate to approach a newbie for fear that the person is not a supporter.

Veteran

The veteran has been with the company the longest and seen how changes have negatively affected the work environment. This individual has great work habits and is the kind of person new workers turn to for help. The veteran remembers the last campaign or back when the company was union.

About to Retire

The about to retire person probably won't sign a card or attend a meeting. He or she has survived countless management changes and doesn't see a reason to make waves. One thing that might convince the about to retire is solidarity with the remaining workers.

178. Know a Few Labor Stats

You don't have to know everything but familiarize yourself with some current labor statistics. How many members does your union have? What's the member count in your local? What's the union density in your state? What's the average pay rate? What's the minimum wage? Knowing these stats and others may help you when trying to communicate with members, future members, and the public.

179. Learn Some Labor Chants

Learn some popular labor chants for rally's, pickets and protests. Practice them with your members and organizing committee. The simpler the chant, the better. Avoid long chants that sometimes confuse people. Customize chants for your campaigns. Bring copies to distribute to participants.

There's always that one boisterous person at a rally we can rely on to get a chant going. These are the same fun individuals who start the wave at stadiums. We should all aspire to be like them.

180. Keep Quiet While Picketing

Instruct all your volunteers to keep quiet while picketing. The picket line is the wrong place to have a conversation with the workers. One wrong word could be costly. This includes members who might be confused and ask you for your recommendation on whether to cross the picket line or not. It's vital that you explain to your volunteers to keep quiet. Some people will have a harder time than others complying with your instructions. It just doesn't seem natural when someone asks a question or says, "Good morning" to not respond. Only the designated "line captain" should do any speaking, and that person should be cautious.

Setting up a picket can be very complex. There are several legal matters that are best decided with the help of a labor attorney. Before picketing, you need to make sure you have all the facts correct to avoid any liability. Who are you picketing against? Are you sure they are at the address? Who is the owner? Which contractor is the general or prime? What subcontractors are there? Where is main entrance? Only after the information is confirmed should you continue planning your activities. You'll need a map of the site or at least a sketch of the area. You should provide copies to all your volunteers and use the map to direct them where to go. Include landmarks such as fences, gates, streets and guard shacks. Plan to recruit twice as many volunteers as you think you will need to ensure you have adequate help. If possible, brief your volunteers before they go to the site so that everyone knows what is expected of them.

You may need to consider logistics, such as parking spaces, money for parking, coffee and doughnuts, nearby restroom facilities, lunch, and signs. People have different opinions about whether you should inform other unions in advance, but it's probably best to keep it a secret. All it takes is one person to ruin a surprise. If others know in advance, they'll schedule the workers on other shifts and the picket won't have the same impact.

There's on exception, depending on the relationship you have with your local police department. If you have good communication with the police, you may want to inform them so they are not blindsided if they receive calls. This communication can make all the difference if accusations are made about anyone in your group causing a disturbance. Labor police officers especially appreciate being told in advance, because it makes them seem like they're "in the know." They can be very helpful at a picket in communicating with their fellow officers and in helping to defuse tense situations.

Use the right sticks when you make your signs. If the stick is thick enough to be used as a weapon, you don't want to use it. Anything larger is a liability. Tape up the handles with clear packaging tape to reduce the risk of splinters. Be sure to have all your people show up early. The trick is to put the line up as the workers arrive. And the shift begins. If you have a successful picket, you may shut down a project with hundreds of workers and cost thousands of dollars in delays. There is a tremendous liability for your local when you picket so err on the side of caution. You may need to get a sanction from Local Building Trades or Central Labor Council if possible. Make sure your signs clearly state why you are picketing the target.

181. Feed Volunteers

The best way to ensure volunteers are happy and productive is to keep them well-fed. Time is our most precious commodity. It's the one thing we can't get more of. Show gratitude to those members and their families who make the effort. Have a variety of snacks on-hand to help shore-up support and enthusiasm. Nothing says we appreciate you donating your time and skills more than an ample supply of food and drinks. If you don't feed volunteers, expect them to slip away as they become hungry. End every effort with a sit-down meal if the budget permits. Take a group photo and share with other members to impress the importance of solidarity. This is a great way to recognize your volunteers and insure more in the future.

For morning events, coffee and doughnuts is a bare minimum. Try to include as many additional snack items as possible. Apples, oranges, granola bars, bottled water, sodas, and tea are popular choices.

Lunchtime events require something more substantial. Pizza's, submarine sandwiches, burritos, fried chicken or hamburgers are go-to items that satisfy. If ordering sandwiches, get them without condiments and allow people to add them as they prefer. Have plenty of snacks and drinks on hand such as cookies, chips, bottled water, sports drinks, and energy drinks.

For dinner, feed volunteers a full meal including a salad and dessert. Keep in mind one very important point, nothing is too good for the members. If we are feeding politicians tri-tip steak, and volunteers hamburger, there's something very wrong.

182. Use Theatrics

One of the most memorable protests in Los Angeles had to be the time Santa and his helpers delivered coal to a naughty CEO. It was a stroke of pure genius! It took place downtown, on a busy street dwarfed by huge towers looming above. A pickup truck pulled up, Santa jumped out and quickly offloaded a wheelbarrow. An empty box was placed inside to displace the charcoal briquettes poured over the box. One or two bags was all it took. They placed a garland around the rim and handles to give it a holiday look. Then off they went. Upon arrival at the entrance, Santa was stopped by security. They weren't about to let the disheveled Santa and his mischievous helpers in the lobby with a wheelbarrow full of coal. There in front of the glass entrance, before a crowd of onlookers, the organizer explained to bewildered security officers, Santa was there to deliver coal to the CEO for mistreating his workers during the Christmas season. Photos and video were taken of the event and later shared online. It was theatrics at its best.

How could you use theatrics to get your point across? Get creative, your volunteers will love it!

183. Back the Business Manager

Progress involves change and change makes people nervous. No matter how much we push back and whine, hoping for the status quo, tough decisions need to be made. Industry requires change. Back the business manager. It's not an easy job.

184. Leave It Better Than It Was

Organizing done right should result in a stronger union, with more members, increased revenues, greater political strength, increases in training, and better safety. If this isn't the case something is seriously amiss. Look around. What needs to be improved?

185. Put Your Heart into It

There's a big difference between doing a job and putting your heart into it. Anyone can dabble in the field for a time, but a true professional will master the process. Put your heart into it and everyone will know.

186. Visit Sick Workers

When we're ill, that's when we find out who has our back. Sometimes even family and friends avoid us. There's the fear of spreading germs, the feeling of helplessness, wanting to give the person some privacy. Some of us just hate hospitals. They remind us of our own vulnerability. None of us look our best when recuperating. The ones who make the effort to visit us when we're sick are cherished.

A friend made visiting sick members a priority. As a business agent, he felt he should. It didn't matter if they were in the hospital or home convalescing. Sometimes people didn't want visitors, but he always tried. He ended up in the hospital himself, for an extended period, after a liver transplant. All of us visited him. Members called and dropped by the hall to ask how he was doing. "Is there anything the family needs," they would ask. Well-wishers sent flowers and cards. It seemed the whole community was praying for him. After a long recovery, he returned to work. His first day back, he was off to visit a sick member.

187. Explore Roads Less Traveled

Literally, explore different routes in the jurisdiction to keep informed of organizing opportunities in the area. Change things up. Take the scenic route. You never know what opportunities you might discover.

188. Focus on Their Interests

When meeting with workers, focus on their interests. Find out what concerns they are experiencing. Learn about their challenges and formulate ways the union can help.

189. Have a Great Attitude

Everything successful comes down to having a great attitude. It can help you through the best and worst of times.

I met a friend for lunch who had just experienced a devastating loss. We hadn't talked in a few years. He was always traveling around the world as a rock star in a major touring band. I called him up and invited him to lunch. He was upbeat and talkative. We joked and laughed. I knew he just lost his position in the band. It might be the end of his music career, but it never came up. He was more interested in hearing about me writing this book! What an amazing guy. What a great attitude to have.

190. Aspire to Give More

If we make helping others and lifting the downtrodden our ardent ambition, giving a little more will come naturally. It won't feel like a burden. We'll be in pursuit of or goal. And when we reach it, we'll aspire to give even more.

191. Become an Ally

Stand up with like-minded community organizations and supporters seeking social justice. Get involved by signing petitions, attending rallies, and donating to worthy causes.

192. Give Generously

Union organizers make decent salaries. We are lucky to be able to do what we truly love and get paid for it. We can probably afford to spread some of it around. Let's not skimp when a member's daughter is selling Girl Scout cookies, or the minority caucus is selling raffle tickets. Be the first to say, "yes." When a member's out-of-work and asks for assistance, be the one to help out. We know what we give will come back to us ten-fold. When they pass the hat around for a sick or injured worker, dig deep. We would want them to do the same for us if we were in their shoes. God loves a cheerful giver. Do it for charities sake. Not because we want people to like us, but because it's the right thing to do.

Often, people will follow other's lead. They were going to give a few bucks, but after seeing you throw in a twenty, they reach in their wallet and do the same. Better yet, be the one who sees the need and takes on the responsibility of starting the effort. Now that's leadership. Let's surprise people with our generosity. Give enough where they say to themselves, "wow! I didn't expect that response." Now that the members are taken care of, why not go out and do the same for the community? Give generously. There's a tremendous need. Let's be more compassionate to one another. Let's see if we can share the holiday spirit in the summer months as well.

193. Be Compassionate

It seems union organizers are naturally compassionate. We support workers as they struggle for dignity and respect in the workplace. We might get jaded a bit after experiencing negativity with certain campaigns. The constant drumbeat of employer lies, and innuendos wears on even the best organizers. Fight the tendency to become indifferent. Get adequate rest and come back ready to practice kindness and compassion.

194. Share Inspirational Quotes

Get inspired by great philosophers and their sage advice. Look for quotes that motivate and inspire. There's a good chance other people will be inspired too. Share quotes when reporting to members. Post them for people to enjoy on social media. Add a favorite to your email signature. Put inspirational quotes up in the hiring hall and organizing bulletin board.

195. Concentrate on Healthy Companies

Focus on organizing healthy companies where members will be rewarded for their work. Healthy companies are always growing, subsequently, they are constantly hiring. They are pushing into new markets, building new locations. When companies aren't growing they're dying. There's no such thing as good enough in business. Someone's always trying to take your lunch. Some businesses don't deserve a bailout. Incompetent management practices, exorbitant CEO pay, failure to anticipate market changes, hostile takeovers, fleecing of the coffers, defaults on financial obligations, these are all catch-phrases for run. Concentrate your efforts on organizing healthy companies and let the others die-on-the-vine.

196. Improve Your Vocabulary

Communicate at a higher level. All of us can gain by improving our vocabulary. It isn't hard to do, but it does take some effort. Add a few new words every month. Practice using them in conversations and in writing. Our vocabulary sends clues to those around us about our education and ability to communicate effectively. Try adding a few vocabulary words every month.

- Propensity

- Juxtapose

- Complacency

- Acquiesce

- Concise

- Parameters

- Cordial

- Scrutinized

- bloviate

- Implication

- Gratuitous

- Complimentary

- Hierarchy

197. Champion Education

"Education is what survives when what has been learned has been forgotten." - *B.F.Skinner*

Champion education and encourage members to continue learning throughout their careers. In doing so, we are advocating for member's career advancement, and standard of living. An educated, well-trained workforce strengthens the union's position in bargaining. We need workers to be aware of occupational hazards and skilled in first-aid techniques and CPR (Cardio Pulmonary Resuscitation). Why stop there? People who have a burning desire to learn should be applauded. What advanced training does your union provide? Take the classes yourself and encourage others as well.

198. Stand Up for Principles

What are your rules? How would we find out? One way is to see if your actions match what you say. Another is to see if you say different things at different times. Some people seem to flop in the wind. Avoid waffling.

199. Provide Letters of Recommendation

Provide letters of recommendation to apprentice candidates and members seeking career advancement. The goodwill we show others will come back to us tenfold. The union should be the very first place workers turn for support. Union organizers who show compassion for those in need will always be appreciated. A simple letter of recommendation can mean the difference between being hired and not being hired. Make the effort.

Twice during my career people have provided recommendation letters. The first was the owner of two companies I worked at. Although my request signaled I would be leaving soon, he tasked his top manager with writing two letters for me. Both were printed on letterhead, each with a different company name. He owned several. It was a kind gesture and I'll always be grateful to him. With those letters, I was accepted into the union apprenticeship program. The other was from a general foreman I worked with. It was so well written I was sure he copied it from a book. I applied for a union scholarship and was denied. Either way, the effort was appreciated.

200. Recognize Genius

Everyone is capable of moments of genius. Recognize genius in others. Look for it. Expect it to manifest in those around us. When we do, we are more open to discovering solutions to everyday challenges.

201. Advocate for Minority Workers

As I wrote in my first book, Bigger Labor, it's more than just a numbers game. It's about individuals working together in unison for a common goal. That's what unions are all about. We need to ensure equal access for jobs, respect for one another, and show recognition of each other's contributions. But it's going to take more than that. The labor movement needs diversity in leadership and staff appointments such as organizing positions.

202. Promote Career Advancement

Always be promoting education, training, and career advancement, even if it means losing a member to management. Better a former member be the manager than an outsider with no experience with the union.

203. Adhere to Good Business Practices

As professional union organizers, we need to adhere to good business practices, such as keeping expenses low and having accurate records. We should know our competitors. Implement a strategic organizing plan. Practice strict confidentiality and uphold the highest ethics.

204. Uncover Corruption

Let's pledge to uncover corruption in our industries. Anything that goes counter to the ideals of organized labor needs to be exposed.

205. Count Maybe's as No Votes

You should ask directly, "can we count on your vote?" If in the process of doing house visits or evaluating worker sentiment, a worker hesitates to state their preference, consider that person a no. Don't try to rationalize the situation. "Well, they invited me in and we spoke for 45 minutes." That's plenty of time for the person to give you an unambiguous "I'm voting Yes!" or "I'm voting no!"

Understand, sometimes people have a hard time saying where they stand. Are they with us or not? We just want a simple answer, but the person may find it easier to appear neutral. That way there's no hard feelings or repercussions.

We see this type of thing happen in the dating scene. Two people make plans on a Saturday night. One person thinks it's a date. The other rationalizes that they are "just friends" seeing a movie and grabbing a bite to eat before the show. Somewhere there's a lack of communication.

206. Create a Candidate Feedback Survey

Do you meet with candidates often? Why not ask for feedback? Create a short candidate feedback survey that reviews the topics covered. How much of the information you provide is retained? Are there some topics that are unclear? Does the person know what the next steps are? Reviewing a feedback survey might be enlightening.

After surveying a few candidates', I realized we needed a checklist for applicants. There were requirements such as photo ID, check stubs to prove hours of experience, and High School diploma or GED, etc. Most people would remember only some of the requirements. The checklist clarified what needed to be provided.

207. Brainstorm for Innovative Ideas

Find the right time for inspiration.

When is your head most clear and your mind free to see things as they should or could be? Are you a morning person or night owl? Are you at your best when you are creating something, in an athletic situation, after a yoga class, when meditating or at some other time? Only you can decide when the time is right.

For me, it's the early morning… there's no need for coffee to wake me up. I love to get out of bed, see the morning dew, and relax in the calmness. On camping trips, I'll get up and go for a long walk, hours before anyone else makes a stir. I can spend hours fishing in complete silence. It's at times like these that everything seems to make sense.

Your ideal time might be completely different from mine. You might get your best insights at the end of the day, in the middle of the night, or after you eat a good meal. Whatever your idea of the right time for inspiration is, that's when you should brainstorm.

It may help you to do deep-belly or diaphragmatic breathing like the kind practiced in yoga or meditation. It's been proven to reduce stress and aid in calming the mind. Simply inhale through your nostrils, drawing in as much air as you can, expanding your abdomen rather than your chest. Place one or both hands on your belly as you do this so that you can feel your diaphragm expand. Hold your breath for a moment, then exhale through your mouth at a slower rate, pushing as much air out as you can. Doing this three or four times should put you in what experts call a "peak state," where your body is relaxed and your mind is free to consider new possibilities.

At this point, you are ready to let the ideas flow. Have a pen and writing pad or alternative available and transcribe every idea that comes to you. Don't worry about whether your ideas are doable or if there's money in the budget or how you are going to accomplish the task, just write. Get all your ideas out. Come up with solutions for your most pressing problems. Ask yourself some difficult questions. How can you get more members to attend your meetings? What would be the best way to attract 50 new members? What topic could you use in a letter to communicate with non-union workers? Is there something you can do to help retain apprentices?

Now that you have your brainstorm list completed. Take a short break and review it at another time. Cross out the ideas that just don't make sense and keep the ones that do. This is how the process of brainstorming works. You can try the same process with a group, just make sure everyone's ideas are considered and no one is criticized for their contributions.

208. Don't Fear Failure

"Do one thing every day that scares you." -Eleanor Roosevelt

Some people quit before they even start. The fear of failure paralyzes them. We should take heed and commit ourselves to push forward. Failure isn't the problem; quitting is. Feel the fear and act anyway.

209. Steeple Your Hands

This simple hand gesture makes one appear more confident and projects power. Steeple your hands by placing fingertips together creating an A-frame. This sends the message you are confident and know what you are talking about. Avoid touching your nose or face which sends the opposite message. Study non-verbal body language to master these techniques.

210. Acknowledge Worker Loyalty

Next time you hand a worker a flyer and the worker reads the word "union" then hands it back, say "you're loyal. We're looking for loyal people like you." Employees are trained by companies and their union busters not to accept literature. They are just doing what they are told to do in this situation. It's company policy, no need to be discouraged. A similar thing might happen in the days and weeks prior to an NLRB election. Therefore, we leave a cushion of around twenty percent over what's needed to win before filing cards. Employees are very loyal to the companies they work for, sometimes to their own detriment. Remember, the company's name is on the worker's paycheck.

In my first book, Bigger Labor; a crash course for construction organizers, I mentioned how we exposed crooked contractors. Even though these owners were underpaying workers, substituting specified materials with cheap imitations, and claiming fewer employees on their workers' comprehensive insurance policy, the workers remained loyal to the end. At times it seems these employers will do anything to save a buck. We are obligated to try to expose these crooks so that legitimate employers can compete on a level playing field.

To help workers, we're going to come across many crooked companies. They are easy to identify. Just keep track of the companies' candidates are leaving, to join the union. At some point, a pattern will appear, and it will become obvious that so many individuals will have similar stories of being cheated, shorted on their checks, or not being paid at all. Most of the time, it's something small like a few hours stolen here or there. However, if the employer feels like they can get away with more they will. When we find companies taking advantage of worker's, it's our obligation as union organizers to expose them. Just remember, current employees, tend to be very loyal.

211. Create an Exit Survey

Find out specifically why members are dropping from the ranks. Use an exit survey to get feedback from outgoing members. If we don't ask, we'll never know why. It's far easier to keep existing members than to constantly organize new ones. There is not enough effort being put forth to quell the exodus. In one union alone; over 20,000 members drop every single month. While a large portion are retired or dead, thousands each month drop for a variety of other reasons.

Here are some likely reasons members are dropping from the ranks:

- Lack of work

- Retirement

- Sickness

- Death

- Lack of communication

- Employers playing favorites

- Transportation issues

- Care for family members

- Travel costs

- Active duty military

- Dues, fines, fees

212. Specialize in Your Field of Organizing

We don't have to be good at every kind of organizing to be successful. If we identify those activities where we are most effective, we can specialize. Focused energy can lead to increased results, better assignments, and more job satisfaction.

We are told by career counselors to "do what you love" and specializing in your field of organizing might be just the thing to ignite that passion. Another advantage to specialization is being able to choose who you work with. In medicine, a general practitioner is trained to care for the entire family, where a specialist in sports medicine cares mainly for athletes. In union organizing, we have specialist's as well. There are organizers who specialize in construction organizing, professional and industrial organizing, government, civil service etc. There are subspecialties by craft; electricians, carpenters, painters, laborers, iron-workers, heat and frost insulators, etc. Then there are subsets of subspecialties such as those who specialize in bottom-up, top-down, salting, mass applications, pickets, bannering, etc. Whatever area of organizing you specialize in, make sure you are passionate about it.

213. Do Your Own Market Assessment

Stay on top of trends to keep ahead of the competition. We are more informed about the industries we work in than most people realize. There's no reason to pay market analysts when so much of the information is available to us for free. Between online research, cursory knowledge of local trends, and conversations with key industry leaders, we're more than capable of formulating our own reliable market assessment. Include variables such as demographics, economy, competition, employment data, trends, and building permits to analyze the overall state of the industry.

214. Up Your Enthusiasm

"People are just as happy as they make up their minds to be." - Abraham Lincoln

When we increase our enthusiasm, we give ourselves an edge. It doesn't take much. A little more enthusiasm goes a long way. When we decide to be more enthusiastic, we aren't just pumping ourselves up. We are raising the energy level for those around us. Some people will fail to notice, but the majority will match our enthusiasm.

215. Write Great Headlines

Use seven words or less on banners, headlines, etc. Push the reader's buttons, create a sense of urgency, spark curiosity, and compel them to act. Pick the best words to describe the topic. Try placing the words in different orders. Don't confuse the reader with too much information.

How to Write a Great Headline

You know you need a great headline. You'll probably only get one chance to make an impression, so you need to take your best shot. If your headline sucks no one will bother to find out more about the issue. A headline with too many words won't get read and one with too much information will lack intensity. A great headline should push the reader's buttons, create a sense of urgency, and compel them to act.

Try these techniques to help you create a great headline:

- Choose the best words – Pick three or four words that describe the topic. Place the words in different order.

  Example #1: Smith Cheated Acme Investors

  Example #2: Acme Investors Cheated by Smith

  Example #3: Investors in Acme Cheated by Smith

- Keep it short – A headline should be brief and to the point. Limit the message to seven words or less.

  Good Example: Acme Refuses to Bargain

Bad Example: Acme Construction Refuses to Bargain in Good Faith

- Keep it simple – Don't confuse the reader with too much info.

- Good Example: John Smith Abuses Workers

  Bad Example: Night Shift Supervisor John Smith Abusive to Female Employees

- Push Their Buttons – Try to get a gut response.

- Example #1: Acme Development Inc. Harms Kids

  Example #2: Acme Development Inc. Bad Neighbors

  Example #3: Acme Development Inc. Cheats Seniors

- Create urgency –You need the reader to act immediately

- Example #1: Stop Construction Now! Call 555-5555

  Example #2: Stop Construction! Call Mayor Smith Today

  Example #3: Stop Construction Before it's too Late!

- Spark Curiosity – Ask a question to get a response

  Example #1: What's Wrong at Acme Canning?

  Example #2: Does Acme Make You Sick?

  Example #3: What Stinks at Acme Canning?

Using the above techniques, here are 3 steps to writing a great headline;

1. Write Three Headlines – Select the one you like the most.

2. Sleep on it – Come back and look at your work in the morning.

3. Get a Second Opinion – Ask a trusted friend or coworker for their input.

If you used these ideas to create your headline you can be confident you will grab people's attention and motivate them to action. You won't confuse people with too much information. You may even spark their curiosity to seek more information about your cause. You're ready to take it to the street. So, get out there and create change!

216. Conduct an Industry Seminar

Whatever industry you are in, there's a need for better seminars and workshops. Conducting an industry seminar is an opportunity for your local union to network with key individuals and decision makers. A well-planned event will attract workers interested in career advancement. Involving popular vendors and industry leaders can increase attendance. Product demonstrations, vendor freebies, and hands-on-training add value to such an event.

217. Create an Action Board

Collect photos and images that provide a sense of urgency to action. Pin images on a bulletin board or glue them in a collage. Many people find this to be helpful in focusing on their goals.

218. Host a Booth at a Job Fair

Represent your union at job fairs and career fairs as an exhibitor. The experience can be fun and exciting. Politicians, celebrities, educators and business leaders are invited to these events and regularly attend to give back to the community. Schools, community centers, churches, veteran groups, institutions all need exhibitors to profile career opportunities to job seekers. Job fairs are a chance to attract and retain members as well as demonstrate to the public what your union offers. Some great networking happens at these events with politicians and career counselors looking to help clients and constituents.

Most job fairs provide a standard 6' or 8' table and chairs. Some industry events will expect you to have a trade show display booth. Regardless of the size or space make the most of the design by planning an eye-catching layout. Even a simple folding table can be transformed with a linen tablecloth and some industry related chachkas. Banners can add to the layout. Have professional quality handouts and business cards ready. Give away some freebies such as custom pens, candies, letter openers, stickers or pins. The minute the event starts, ditch the chairs under the table. Attract the most candidates by upping your energy level and showing enthusiasm.

Police, fire, military, and municipalities are regulars at job fairs regardless of the economy. Others often seen are insurance companies, financial services, and universities. Unfortunately, many companies use job fairs to promote their brand instead of a way to recruit candidates to fill positions. Talk about rubbing salt in the wound of the unemployed. Don't do that. Only host a booth at a job fair if there are positions to fill.

Creativity really pays off when it comes to booths at job fairs. The union's training facility hosted a booth at an electrical industry event. On display was a Jacob's Ladder like the ones seen in old Frankenstein movies. The arc of electricity rising from the electrodes was hypnotizing and attracted a crowd. Later a pipe bending demonstration was done with volunteers who had never performed that type of work before. They were very enthusiastic and received prizes for participating.

219. Provide Candidates with a Study Guide

If there is a placement exam prior to entering the apprenticeship program, provide a free study guide. Make sure all the information is up-to-date. A study guide should help a candidate prepare, as well as ease anxiety many people experience before being tested. Include an answer sheet and time limit so the person can judge if they are ready. A study guide should not include exact questions but give a general idea of the concepts covered on the exam itself.

220. Control Your Emotions

Control your emotions and keep cool under pressure. It's a sure sign of maturity. Coworkers able to control their emotions are less likely to lash out when things get tough. Nothing phases them. It's a pleasure to work with such professionals. They've always got your back.

Have you ever noticed how some people relish drama? They love the highs and curse the lows, all-the-while secretly enjoying the chaos. Try to avoid people like that whenever possible.

221. Start a Mentoring Program

Sometimes there are barriers to membership. A mentoring program can help interested candidates gain the knowledge or skills to get in. Maybe it's as simple as needing someone to go over the application process, or a translator, or financial help, perhaps a candidate needs a math refresher, or practice performing a mechanical aptitude test. A mentoring program can increase the number of eligible candidates.

222. Provide Apprentices with Donated Tools

Hand-tools and work clothes can be expensive, especially for new apprentices. Consider having a drop-box in the hiring hall where members can donate used tools or work clothes. Ask retired members to donate their old tools. Provide donated tools to apprentices who can't afford to buy their own. Remember to thank members who donate. Their generosity will encourage the next generation of members.

223. Connect New Members with Sponsors

A sponsor can be any member willing to take an active role to mentor a new member to success. Connect new members with sponsors for better retention. New members require personal attention.

224. Warn People Against Giving Two-Week Notice

Giving two-week notice can be risky for workers.

Two Week Notice; Best Practice or Risky Move?

Over the years providing employers two weeks' notice when quitting has become commonplace. There are things to consider however when making the decision to give notice. It may be required in situations where a contract is in force, but in most cases, it's just a courtesy to the employer.

In a professional work environment, it's easy to understand why providing an employer time to locate and train a replacement is important. In this way, production goes on and hopefully doesn't negatively affect the company or coworkers. In most cases, two weeks should be enough for a business to find a replacement.

There are many things to consider when resigning from a job. These decisions will affect whether to provide notice or not. Maybe the person found work that is more appealing, or decided to go back to school, or are fleeing a hostile work environment. Here are some things a worker should consider when contemplating giving the employer two weeks' notice.

- Will the current employer be used for references?

- Is there any chance of returning in the future?

- Will the worker be dealing with the employer again in the future?

- Has the person earned paid vacation time?

- Would the person consider staying if offered more money or a promotion?

Beware, employers often choose to terminate an employee who gives notice. Reasons vary from fear of the person spreading discontent, to loss of momentum due to what they call "short-timers disease." After all, if the person is not happy in the position, how effective will they be?

225. Familiarize Yourself with the Department of Veteran's Affairs

The United States Department of Veterans Affairs or VA is a federal agency providing military veterans with benefits and services. Extended federal unemployment and college education benefits are available to veterans. The VA supports veterans after they serve, with a budget of over $275 billion dollars, and employs over 375,000 people.

226. Seek More Responsibilities

"Yesterday's home runs don't win today's games." - **Babe Ruth**

Become more valuable as an organizer, seek more responsibilities. Take on new projects and assignments. Offer to assist overworked colleagues.

Once, while working as an apprentice electrician, my journeyman said, "let's be so busy when they come to lay us off they won't find us."

227. Provide Toys or Coloring Books for Candidate's Kids

When members or candidates meet with you, they will sometimes bring their young children. It can be difficult for a parent, to fill out paperwork or carry a conversation, if their child is crying or fidgety. Ask the parent if it's ok to give the child a small toy or coloring book. Be the hero of the situation.

228. Send Thank You Cards

People love feeling appreciated and sending a thank you card says we are grateful. It also reminds the person of meeting us. In a busy, fast-paced society like ours, sending thank you cards is needed now more than ever. It's a simple way to connect with people. Some don't know what to write. Just be brief and to the point. "Councilmember Cole, thank you for meeting with us about paid family leave. Sincerely."

229. Call Workers During Lunch or After Hours

Let's not risk causing workers trouble with their employers. Return calls during their lunch break or after hours if possible.

230. Assist Workers with Resumes

A second set of eyes can make the difference between a good resume and an outstanding one. Help spot errors and omissions workers might overlook. Be a resource and a trusted advisor to both the unemployed and high-climbers.

231. Maximize Attendance at Union Meetings

Try new ways to maximize attendance at union meetings. Serve delicious food, give away door prizes, raffle off awesome prizes, post meeting minutes under glass vs reading them allowed, recognize members for their years of service, invite retirees, add a color guard, honor military veterans, invite spouses to attend, ask politicians to address the members. Provide union stewards with buttons that read, "Meeting Tonight." There are dozens of ways to increase attendance and make union meetings more fun. As organizers, it's our job to convince members to attend their meetings.

232. Request Referrals

Be a sponge for member referrals. Distribute flyers and business cards in the community. Write letters to local colleges and career counselors seeking candidates. Never refuse a referral even in a bad economy. The least we can do is meet with an individual and offer guidance. Many organizers wait until work is plentiful and candidates are scarce to begin recruiting efforts. There's often a lag time between the organizer putting out the word and people responding. Instead, always be refining your list of interested candidates.

233. Use a Personal Logo

There are many online services that offer inexpensive custom designed logos. Order a logo of your name and use it on leaflets and promotional materials. A well-designed personal logo will position you as the go-to organizer in your industry.

234. Find Your Cause

What drives you? Is there an issue you're passionate about? Is there something you would like to improve on? What do you do in your spare time? Find your cause and run with it!

235. Pick Your Battles

The Board Agent says you can bring two Observers. You want to bring three. Is it worth arguing about? Step back and see the big picture. Pick your battles wisely.

236. Look for Warning Signs

Keep an eye out for tell-tale signs something isn't right. People don't always communicate what they are thinking. They will sometimes tell you exactly what you want to hear.

237. Make People Feel Important

"Always trust the rank and file. They will make the right decisions." - Harry Bridges

They are important! Build them up. Acknowledge other's contributions. Take time to connect and listen to what people have to say. Make others the center of attention. It makes life easier when we screw up or need to cut out early.

238. Don't Knock their Employer

Workers are extremely loyal to the company they work for. Over the years, through good times and bad, people become very close. A job can be like family at times. Coworkers rely on one another, their families and friendships. Don't forget, the boss writes their paycheck. For these reasons and more, don't knock their employer.

239. Invite Don't Sell

Invite workers to join the union, don't sell them on the idea. People feel good about being invited, but they may feel resentment at being sold something. No matter how convincing you are, don't be pushy. Give meaning to people's lives by inviting them to be part of something great.

240. Seek Alternative Views

What are the other arguments? Do a quick survey to find out. Allow dissenting views. Listen carefully. Sometimes we find our views are not in line with those of the group. Find out before problems arise.

241. Recover Quickly

Bounce back after a loss. Shake it off and move forward to avoid getting in a funk.

242. Save Your Money

Take control of your own finances and save for retirement. Lead by example. Be more effective when speaking to others about their financial situation by securing yours. There's a feeling of contentedness that comes with having a nest egg. Living paycheck-to-paycheck leaves us feeling anxious and unsettled. The rain is going to come eventually, in the form of financial setbacks and unexpected challenges. Be prepared and help others as well.

243. Speak Slowly

Studies have proven people who speak slowly are perceived to be more intelligent than those who talk fast. If we can appear to be smarter by simply speaking slower, why not give it a try?

244. First Organize Your Office

Some people's offices are so cluttered, there's no way they can be at their best. First organize your office, then organize the jurisdiction. At the beginning of each year, clear out unnecessary files and outdated materials. Do some Spring cleaning. Empty your inbox and voicemails.

245. Make Your Bed

A Princeton University study found, the more cluttered a room the more difficult it is to concentrate. Make your bed and start the day right. Navy SEALs do it. You want to argue with them? Go ahead.

246. Listen to Council

To become an attorney takes a minimum of 7 years of college, a law degree and passing the state bar exam. Most of us spent too much time examining the inside of a bar to pass an exam. Listen to council and let them buy the drinks.

247. Solve Other's Problems

Solve other's problems including the boss. Make yourself a valuable member of the team. Don't wait to be asked. Surprise people by taking initiative.

248. Cut Down on Clutter

Make cutting down on clutter a regular part of your routine. Empty out the desk and shred some documents. The same goes for the computer desktop.

249. Get Used to Rejection

Do we ever really get used to rejection? Yes. It gets a whole lot better after having a few doors slammed in our face and people walking by ignoring us when hand billing. That doesn't mean we won't get a few butterflies in our stomach tomorrow when we start again. We get used to it and we keep on going.

250. Set Realistic Deadlines

Union organizing was never a sprint. If anything, union organizing is a marathon. By making daily consistent progress, we prevail. Careful not to overdo it when setting deadlines.

251. Show Your Union Pride

Put a union sticker on your car. Wear union t-shirts, hats, and jackets. Post union activities online. Place labor candidate's signs in your yard. Attend union meetings, annual picnics, and events.

252. Meet with Other Organizers

Schedule regular meetings with union organizers in and around your area. Exchange ideas for collaboration and support. Don't be an island unto yourself. We are stronger together.

253. File Before Noon

File RC Petitions before Noon for maximum results. We want the filing with the National Labor Relations Board to catch the employer off guard and to move forward immediately. Delays give employers more time to interrogate workers and conduct captive audience meetings. Sometimes a board agent will have questions about a filing. By filing in the morning, you are insuring adequate time to answer any questions needed. Your petition will be finished by end of business day to get the clock ticking.

254. Don't Ask for an Extension

When Representation Petitions are filed, employers often start committing Unfair Labor Practices. There's a tendency to circle the wagons and be defensive or worse, get litigious. Delays heavily favor the employer. Don't ask for an extension.

255. Pull the Petition If You Sense a Loss

Some think we owe it to the workers to take it to a vote regardless of the outcome. You've heard the saying, "it's better to have tried and lost then to never have tried?" They're wrong. Losing a union organizing campaigns sucks! The idea that, "we'll get them next year" is a farce. We might not get another chance. What if workers lose interest, they quit, get fired, or are retaliated against? A loss shows management the group isn't united. A loss tells workers the union organizers are amateurs. No need to candy coat it.

Go over the list of eligible voters with the volunteer organizing committee members. Tally votes from information gathered during house calls and face-to-face commitments. Take into consideration situations affecting supporters such as, out on sick leave and on vacation, etc. Count every undecided as a no. Don't get mired in the weeds with explanations like, "leaning yes" or "leaning no." Take your best guess.

256. Create Transitional Agreements

It can be complicated for an employer to become union overnight. A transitional agreement helps employers immerse themselves into union culture over time, not instantaneously. Creating a transitional agreement can insure a smooth, more harmonious transition for both the company and union.

257. Lawyer Up

Schedule in advance to have a lawyer available during the NLRB Election process. Things happen fast, and quick responses are needed. Don't just assume. Make the call, so the attorney knows to free up time if necessary.

258. Get Employer's Email Address Early

Early in the process of meeting with workers, get the employer's email address. Sometimes it can be found on the company website. Don't let not having information cause a delay in filing with the NLRB.

259. Do a Resume Search

Several online services such as indeed.com allow you to do a resume search by title, city, state, company, zip, employer or job classification. These services can be used to develop a list of workers at a given company both past and present.

260. Write a Post-Political Campaign Overview

Take notes while working on city, state, and presidential political campaigns. Note what worked and what didn't. Compare campaign strategies and tactics. Who stayed on point and drove the message home? Who got mired in the weeds and went off topic? Which candidate appeared calm under fire? Write a post-political campaign overview to help better understand election results.

261. Form a Decertification Response Team

Form a decertification response team, before there is a problem. Assign duties that compliment participant's strengths. Conduct house calls and phone members. Get to the bottom of complaints before they become problems. The number one complaint by employees during decertification campaigns is, "we never heard from our representatives."

Decertification's affect everyone. The ripple-effect hurts current and future organizing campaigns. When unions service members correctly and cater to worker's needs, no one wants to leave. Train job stewards to be more effective. Have them report often. Pay attention to complaints by members and keep communication open. Well-informed members are happy members.

262. Ask Follow-Up Questions

When speaking with workers, ask follow-up questions. The more questions we ask the more likely we are to get the information needed. Keep the conversation going. There's a nugget of information in there somewhere.

263. Form a First Contract Negotiating Team

First contracts are tough to negotiate. Skilled negotiators with proven track records can help. Recruit the best people available. Form a first contract negotiating A-Team. Management relies on highly paid attorneys with Ivy League educations to form their team. No wonder attempts by labor to negotiate first contracts often run into resistance. Let's fight back!

264. Give Notice in Advance of Local's Activities

Consider informing members and labor cops prior to any type of picketing or demonstrating. Nothing's worse than seeing your own members cross a picket line. Often, it's caused by a lack of communication.

265. Make Periodic Unscheduled Appearances

Make visits to workers random and often. Be the familiar face of the union. Show up unannounced and look around. You might be surprised what you find.

266. Stand Out from the Crowd

Excel past other's expectations. Put your stamp on the industry by using new techniques and strategies that set you apart. Break out from the mold of a union organizer who doesn't last long, never really accomplishes much, and leaves no legacy. The competition doesn't want us to be noticed. Would you rather blend in and be out of work in two years or stand out and experience the rewards of a successful organizing career? The choice is yours.

267. Use Community Pressure

Use community pressure as leverage against management's nefarious activities. Companies are concerned about public perception. Push back and use their concern as your strength.

268. Learn About Card-Check Agreements

With a card check agreement in place, a simple majority of interested workers who sign authorization cards win union representation. Learn how card check can make joining a union easier and familiarize yourself with the arguments against it as well.

269. Research Companies in Advance

Before meeting with a group of workers to discuss organizing opportunities, research the company. Do an online search and check the company's website. Find out who the key players are and what leverage the union might have. Have there been previous attempts to unionize the workers? Find out in advance.

270. Speak in Sound Bites

If you are contacted by the media, speak in short sound bites. Avoid long drawn out explanations. Help people understand by not using jargon. Practice your delivery.

271. Be Polite and Respectful

Momma taught us right. Be polite and respectful when dealing with people. It's amazing how often we interact with the same individuals. Reputations are formed by our interactions.

272. Understand Before Criticizing

"We have two ears and one tongue so that we would listen more and talk less."
– Diogenes

Don't be too quick to dismiss ideas or criticize. All of us have something useful to contribute. Disagreement in a group can be constructive if we are tactful, and in the end, consensus is met.

273. Create Worker Loyalty

Once workers see our dedication and willingness to serve, they will want to work with us. Create worker loyalty by being so responsive they wouldn't think of meeting with a competing union. Stick with the campaign from start to finish. Be available to answer questions and respond to concerns.

274. Hire Superstars

People who were successful in the past are more likely to be successful in the future. If you are in a position to hire and fire; stick with superstars and top producers. Stop playing amateur hour.

Have you seen this trend? A new organizer is hired with zero background and no education in union organizing. We look for clues for what qualities the person doing the hiring saw and can't figure it out. Are they exceptional communicators? No. Do they have above average job skills? No. Were they active in the local union? No. Is the person exceptionally passionate about union organizing? No. The first six months the newbie fumbles around looking like a deer in the headlights. Eventually, they catch-on and begin making progress. A few years in, they get canned and go back to their previous work. Soon another amateur gets hired and the trend continues. It's a no-win, bound-to-fail proposition and it's killing our unions.

275. Apply What You've Learned

The training given union organizers at conferences, seminars, in books, newsletters, and tapes, won't help unless put into practice. Action is what's needed most. Never mind if someone tried and failed in the past. New techniques and strategies can lead to success. Apply one thing you've learned today.

276. Create a 30-Day Action Plan

A 30-day action plan should be enough to kickstart any organizing effort. It should be flexible enough in case more urgent priorities take precedence. There should be benchmarks to gauge if the plan is working.

277. Mute Phone During Conference Calls

Do participants a favor, mute your phone. Many conference calls are ruined because one or more people leave their microphone hot while they drive or are interrupted. I've personally been on conference calls that have been canceled due to someone causing background noise without the person's knowledge.

There was an important conference call between union organizers for a national campaign. At the given time, we called the number provided and introduced ourselves. The host welcomed the participants and the meeting began. Not long afterward, we realized there was background noise causing distractions. The host and participants had to stop to try and figure out who was causing the distraction. Someone was driving at the time with the window open. The wind hitting the diaphragm of the mic caused an intolerable distraction. That wasn't all. We could hear a rooster in the background! Obviously, the rooster sound was coming from another person's phone. Eventually, the conference call resumed.

278. Decide What Your Contribution Will Be–

"Do not go where the path may lead, go instead where there is no path and leave a trail." - Ralph Waldo Emerson

The masses move in a pack. This is the path that leads to everything that is average. People seldom become exceptional doing things like everyone else. There's that saying, "go big or go home," and it relates to union organizing. If we don't plan on accomplishing great things, we'll settle for mediocrity. That's boring. There's a whole world out there just waiting to be organized.

Many of us love the work we do. Each day presents an opportunity to hone our skills. This work isn't just a job, it's our life's calling. If we hit the lottery, we might still do it. There was a time when I thought such people were crazy. It's not a symptom of delusion. The people who are crazy are the people who get up every day going to a job they hate, spending their lives working for the weekend when the weekend never lasts long enough.

While working as a local organizer, there appeared to be a need for a photographer to capture various labor activities we were involved with. Photography was a hobby of mine, so I began documenting these events. No one asked me to do it. It certainly wasn't in my job description. There were some who questioned my motives. Once everybody settled down, they began to see me as a resource. The secretary needed photos for the newspaper, a business rep wanted pictures for a flyer, members wanted pictures from the picnic. More and more requests started coming in. "Bob! Get over here! We need you to take a picture." Eventually, I was appointed Press Secretary. It wasn't a position I asked to do. It just seemed to make sense. Obviously, I like writing, no one else was taking photos on a regular basis. At one point I thought to myself "Isn't it funny my photos are being published in newspapers, magazines, newsletters, brochures, organizing materials and websites and I'm getting paid to do it?" Pretty good for someone who never took a photography class. What will your contribution be?

279. Get Uncomfortable

Whether we find ourselves in unfamiliar situations, changing direction because of market changes, unforeseen circumstances, or even tasked with new assignments, the idea of change can be frightening. It can cause us to doubt our abilities and cause anxiety. At the same time, we know that we must get out of our comfort zone and embrace change. It's where all growth comes from, and not all change is bad. The same forces that threaten to sap our energy can also revitalize it. There will always be things to fear, obstacles to get in the way or people who will try to trip us up. Instead of letting these things get in the way, let's be motivated by them.

When we are doing something we really love, the benefits will follow. The new way will pay off eventually, perhaps with different rewards. When we create a life that is in line with what we really want to do, the rest comes naturally. We're going to be better at what we do, not just putting in time.

280. Resolve Conflicts

To see an organizing campaign from start to fruition we need to resolve conflicts quickly before they get out of hand. Maybe an early supporter distrusts a latecomer, or two people can't work together, or a VOC member goes rouge. If you are like most of us, you'd rather ignore the situation, hoping it will fix itself. That can be costly in today's workplace, where a single text could change the course of a campaign. The best way to handle the situation is often head-on.

The first thing to do is analyze the situation carefully. Gather as much information as you can. What are the known facts? Identify the source of the conflict, but don't just assume to understand the situation. Be careful not to place blame. This is where some get themselves into trouble. Keep an open mind while brainstorming about what the solution could be.

Most of us were not taught how to resolve conflict in school, though we may have done it in the schoolyard. There are online conflict resolution training courses for those interested. The skills are needed by attorneys, business agents, human resource professionals and others likely to be involved in mediation.

A lot of conflicts in the workplace can be avoided by having clear job descriptions and a collectively bargained contract. Luckily for the unrepresented, the union is interested in resolving their conflicts.

281. Repeat Their Name

Sometimes we forget a person's name soon after being introduced. It can be embarrassing. By repeating their name during a conversation, we make them feel important and it helps us recall the name later. Try using the person's name at least three times in a conversation.

282. Take Notes

Take notes when meeting with workers to show you are listening and to help recall important facts. Ask for permission first. Make sure it's clear any information is confidential and won't be shared with the employer.

283. Affiliate with Employee Associations

Identify employee associations interested in affiliating with your union. Employee associations often lack financial resources, legal expertise and staff needed to adequately represent their members. Some associations even give management the final say in disciplinary decisions. It's no wonder so many members of employee associations contact unions for assistance during negotiations.

Sometimes a small group of skilled workers with training and education will want to break away from a larger group of workers where no training or education is required. Unfortunately, this is difficult to do. There's no upside for less skilled workers allowing the more skilled workers to leave.

For an affiliation campaign to be successful, make sure there aren't any existing mergers either state, local or national before proceeding to avoid trouble with another union. Request a copy of the Collective Bargaining Agreement, Local Rules, M.O.U.'s, (Memorandum of Understanding) and Bylaws. Read the documents thoroughly to get an understanding of how the association represents the bargaining group and what scope of work it covers. Once satisfied that the association is not affiliated with another union, it's safe to proceed.

Initial meetings can be scheduled with association officers. If affiliation is desired, a special meeting with the association members is called to discuss a merger. The union may be invited to give a presentation, afterward a member can make a motion for the association to affiliate with the union. A vote can be taken. A majority supporting an affiliation is all that is required. An affiliation agreement is signed, and a letter is penned to management informing them of the fact. The new group and its officers become a part of the local union with the name and collective bargaining agreement in place.

284. Eat for Energy

There are many benefits to eating healthy and watching our waistlines. One of these benefits is having more energy for the task at hand. It's easy to fall into a rut when our schedules are loaded with responsibilities. Healthy alternatives aren't always immediately available. It's these times when we need to plan ahead or at minimum take into consideration how the food and drinks we consume affect our mood and energy levels. The culprits are the grease, sugar, salt, and preservatives so prevalent in our diets.

To help in fighting the urge to routinely grab a burger, fries and a soda or the doughnut and double latte, stop to ask yourself, "Will this give me more energy or less?" Another question is, "How will eating or drinking this make me feel three hours from now?" If the answer is anything but "energized" look for an alternative. Plan to snack on something more satisfying by bringing your own food including fresh fruit, carrots, and nuts. Drink water or sparkling water instead of caffeinated drinks.

Have you noticed how much free food is available to union organizers? It seems like every meeting, event, or campaign has doughnuts, pastries, sodas and candy in high quantities. While heading out to precinct walk they hand us a bag of salty, sugary snacks. While traveling out-of-town, there's the meal allowance. A last-minute meeting takes place and we wolf down three slices of cheese pizza and a large soda, perhaps four slices if it's free. At the conference reception, there's a complimentary buffet with a full bar. Coworkers who don't consume alcohol give away their drink tickets to those who do. Is it any wonder we sometimes find ourselves overindulging and feeling sluggish?

There was a time when I suffered from heartburn and acid reflux daily. I was overindulging on spicy foods and eating jumbo portions. It caused discomfort during the day and loss of sleep at night. What finally made me aware of the seriousness of the problem was when a coworker brought me a huge oversized bottle of antacid tablets from a warehouse store. He had gotten tired of hearing me complain about needing antacids. The moment he handed me the bottle I realized it was time to talk with my doctor. The doctor made some recommendations and soon the problem was solved. Now I eat for energy and control portions to avoid feeling sluggish.

285. Master Speaking Tone

How we sound when speaking influences our ability to organize. Do we sound whiny or authoritative? Are we enthusiastic or bored? Sometimes when people hear their voices recorded, they are surprised by what they hear. It sounds different in some way.

We can work to improve or speaking tone by practicing reading aloud and emphasizing words to show enthusiasm. People who speak in a monotone voice often sound bored. Record yourself to find out.

286. Don't Be Wormy

"Wormy" is a term used in the construction field, to describe a co-worker who breaks down conditions of employment. An example might be someone who skips breaks or works overtime without reporting it to the employer. It has a ripple effect. Soon, the boss expects everyone to work through breaks and give an extra hour without pay. Peer pressure to bend-the-rules on small things snowballs into something bigger. An example might be; the union negotiates to have employees supply small hand-tools. A guy decides on his own to start bringing large power tools that aren't on the tool list. Another guy brings those and more. A third guy, scared for his job, shows up with his own utility truck full of power tools he leased over the weekend. He figures if there's a lay-off, the boss is likely to keep him because he's got more tools. Where does it end? Don't be wormy. Stick to the contract and don't break down conditions for others.

287. Tell Them Why You Are Unique

How are you unique from other union organizers in the industry? Why should someone choose to work with you? Aren't all unions the same? Make a short list of your outstanding qualifications and achievements. Add advantages your union offers over other unions. Don't keep it a secret. Tell them why you are uniquely positioned to help them succeed.

288. Create Your System

Never mind my system of union organizing or anyone else's. Create your system, the one that works best for you. Make it cost effective, efficient and fun.

There's a scene in the movie, "The Founder" starring Michael Keaton. Ray Kroc and the McDonald brothers are in a parking lot. They have all the employee's doing a mock lunch rush to analyze their productivity. It's pure genius! Every industry needs to analyze their processes for improvement.

289. Pack Disinfecting Wipes

Use disinfecting wipes and hand sanitizer when traveling to kill germs and avoid getting sick. We aren't as effective when we're sick and feeling under the weather. Breathing is difficult, muscles and joints hurt, then there's the fever and cough. Airports, planes, hotel rooms and public restrooms are teaming with contagions that cause such symptoms. There's so much we can do to prevent the spread of germs. We can give ourselves an edge over other travelers by combating the problem head-on. Wipe down common surfaces with disinfecting wipes, especially those likely to be touched repeatedly. Wash hands often and apply hand sanitizing gel. Keep hands away from the nose and eyes.

A local news team did an expose on dirty hotel rooms. They took samples from common items at a national chain. They found television remotes were the most germy items, followed by light switches and bathroom sinks. Armed with this knowledge, we can take preventative measures to sanitize items of concern. It only takes a few minutes. Feeling good and being healthy is the pay-off.

290. Play Music in Your Office

Music can help us be more productive by relieving tension and increasing concentration. It's especially beneficial for people who suffer from Attention Deficit Disorder. Someone once recommended classical music by Johann Sabastian Bach to help with concentration during studying. I tended to listen to punk rock, which would explain my poor grades in high school.

At an office in Washington DC, there was soft music playing in the background. I recognized it as Bach. The gentleman I spoke with, talked in a calm voice as if he didn't have a care in the world. It made me feel at ease. The conversation that followed was like a fire-side chat not wanting to wake nearby campers. I thought to myself, "from now on, I'm playing music in the office." As soon as my flight landed in Los Angeles I was off to shop for speakers.

291. See it from Their Perspective

Part of having empathy for others is to see things from their perspective. We each have different experiences in life. Our own biases can keep us from connecting with others. To have close personal relationships we need to put our own ego in-check. Consider other perspectives and see it from their side.

292. Affirm Your Actions

Union organizing is a noble profession. We lift the downtrodden and honor their work. The rich dismiss unions as insignificant. Speak of your work in positive affirming language. We must convince ourselves, before convincing others.

293. Correspond with Inmates

"The greatest pleasure I know is to do a good action by stealth, and to have it found out by accident." - Charles Lamb

Sometimes the incarcerated reach out to unions for help, before transitioning back into the workforce. Take the opportunity to assist inmates. Provide information on apprenticeship and other training opportunities. Offer to help the individual find employment upon release.

294. Market Your Skills and Abilities

Why be the best-kept secret in town? Take every class you can. Make your resume bullet-proof. Post your skills online for everyone to see. Show up to every union meeting and speak! Be so good the next administration must hire you.

295. Be a Resource for Information

There are a lot of ways to become a resource for information. When we build a reputation for knowing a given topic, people seek our guidance. Gather the information together and share it with others, thereby cementing yourself as an expert.

Throughout my career, I've managed to stay busy. Even in hard times, and there's been a few, work seemed to be plentiful. I began to analyze what worked and what didn't, to help those who came to me for answers. After contemplating the subject, I wrote a series of articles that have helped hundreds of workers remain gainfully employed. The following is the most popular. It appeared in trade publications and was used by instructors to help struggling apprentices be more employable. Though you may be in a different industry the information might be useful to you.

Ten Tips for Staying Employed

Ever wonder why some manage to work year-round while others bounce from employer to employer? "What's their secret?" you might ask. Are they just lucky? Perhaps, but there are some things you can do to even the odds.

Did you know that most Foremen know who they are going to let go weeks before they ever hand out a pink slip? It's a standard practice to make a "Lay off List" with the names of the workers on a crew in order of production. Call it a "Lay off List," a "Head Count," a "Totem Pole"– call it whatever you like, but you're on it. The real question is, "Are you on the top or the bottom?"

Often a Foreman will be told, "Lay off three workers" and given only a moment to make the decision. The names on the bottom are the first to go. You may not be aware that it's a fluid list and that names move up and down as production increases and decreases. It's not just productivity that plays a role in who stays or who goes; let's not kid ourselves, obviously, there's room for prejudices and cronyism to take place as well, but we won't get into that now.

By the way, the Foreman's not the only one deciding who stays and who goes. It may be a Project Manager or even a customer that may see us leaning against a ladder and make a split- second evaluation of our work ethic. It's not fair. That's for sure, but unless our reputation as hard workers precede us, it might be too late for anyone to step in and save us.

Some will work on many jobsites and somehow manage to miss the layoffs. Is it because they're luckier than the next person? No. It's just that they know the ten tips for staying employed.

1. Walk with a Purpose – Get in the habit of walking with a purpose. Don't meander around.

2. Pack a Lunch – We'll save money. We'll eat healthier and when the lunch truck doesn't show it won't matter.

3. Show up Every Day – Even average workers will outlast those who don't.

4. Show up On Time – This one really pays.

5. Be Flexible – Be prepared to do any task assigned.

6. Update your Skills – Take industry related courses.

7. Be Reachable – Use voicemail and return calls quickly.

8. Have Reliable Transportation – Buy the best running vehicle you can afford.

9. Have a Positive Attitude – There's no such thing as "can't".

10. Look the Part – Dress like a professional. You only get 30 seconds to make that first impression.

Well, there it is; ten tips for staying employed. They may seem obvious, but if that's the case why are so many workers caught in the rut of constantly being let go? If we're fortunate enough to work with some of the best in the field, we'll notice that they seem to have these qualities. Consider yourself lucky. Not everyone has the pleasure of apprenticing with such professionals. If we follow these simple steps, we will stay employed longer, earn more money and avoid having to tell our family that the holidays are going to be tight this year. Still, it's a good idea to save a little money for those slow periods.

Do you know someone who's in need of a little guidance, perhaps a new apprentice or even a journeyman who just can't seem to stay employed? Why not take a moment to share this knowledge that might help that person reach their full potential?

296. Hold a Pre-Deposition Conference

Seek council of an attorney and take their advice. Go over the case in advance to gain an understanding of both side's arguments. Be prepared to answer any questions that might come up, clearly and truthfully. Depositions can be intrusive and last for hours or in some cases days. Ask your attorney any questions you might have up front. The constant probing can be unsettling.

297. Ask for a Second Opinion

Sometimes even labor attorneys try to gouge unions. It's a shame, but it happens. If something doesn't add up, ask another attorney for a second opinion. It could save the union a lot of time and money.

298. Find Your Flaw

It's right there, staring us in the face. That one minor flaw. The one that if not taken care of could cause so much grief. It seems everyone can see it but us. We could ask friends or trusted coworkers. We could do some self-evaluation. There's bound to be some clues.

There was an organizer who enjoyed a cocktail in the evening. Soon "a cocktail" became two, then three, then four. This routine went on for months. Mondays were anyone's guess if the organizer would even show up. Everyone knew about it, but no one said a word. It was relatively under control until the business trip to Las Vegas. Then it turned into a full-scale bender. That was the final straw.

299. Look for Conflicts of Interest

The slightest impropriety in the way a company does business might be enough to tilt opinion in the union's favor. Look for conflicts of interests and leverage; managers dating subordinates, relatives getting special treatment, double sets of books, vendors giving certain people special treatment, etc.

300. Prepare for Testimony

Those testifying in court or with an NLRB Agent should prepare by taking time to refresh their memory. Review all documents, photographs, and work schedules. Speak clearly and be sure to understand the question before answering.

301. Equip Your Replacement

Moving on to greener pastures? Retiring? Going back to work in the field? Equip your replacement with the information needed to succeed. As an apprentice, I clearly remember there were some journeymen who refused to train apprentices. They were scared they might be training their replacement. Luckily those individuals were few.

I will always be grateful for professionals who were not afraid to take a newbie under their wing and teach them a trade. The same for the organizers who later were mentors, teaching me union organizing.

There's a disturbing reality in local union politics, regimes get ousted and sometimes organizers get canned regardless of their effectiveness. It can lead to hurt feelings, lost friendships and lost organizing campaigns. Some organizers fail to pass along vital information to their replacement or worse destroy files. Don't be afraid to train new organizers or mentor members interested in union organizing. Commit to leaving the local union in much better shape than the day you joined. Commit to equipping your replacement.

302. Associate with Champions

"The key is to keep company only with people who uplift you, whose presence calls forth your best." – Epictetus

When we perform with champions, they challenge us to get better. Champions want to be stretched and challenged. We all want to work with the best-of-the-best. Keep your eyes open for fun, successful individuals to associate with. Work to improve yourself so others will want to work with you.

303. Talk About Solutions

"Success is not final; failure is not fatal: it is the courage to continue that counts." – Winston Churchill

Challenges are a daily occurrence in union organizing. We need to be upbeat and ready to talk about solutions. There's never just one. Be the person to offer three or four possibilities.

304. Tell Clean Jokes

Some of us don't tell jokes, though it would probably be a good idea to know one or two in a pinch. Others are always cracking people up with their salty wit. Then there's the pranksters and their antics. In today's workplace environment, the potential for someone getting offended has skyrocketed. The slightest infraction by a co-worker can cause an entire crew their livelihood. A dirty joke might have the potential to derail an organizing campaign as well, or at least put the union on defensive.

305. Become a Trusted Advisor

The more success we experience; the more people will seek our advice. Become a trusted advisor to other organizers. Share knowledge and skills freely with other unions and activists. Your reach can far exceed your current jurisdiction. Many of the strategies we rely on as union organizers can be used to advance social justice causes. The world is hungry for empowering thoughts and ideas. Become a trusted advisor and share your expertise.

306. Learn Why Others Fail

This is the great secret that can catapult a union organizing career. Watch, listen, learn why others fail. Evaluate what is being done and said. Look for clues. Who had the most compelling case? What was the fatal flaw? Don't do that.

307. Finish Projects

Anyone can start a project. The real challenge is to see it through to its fruition, put your stamp of approval on it, and finish the job. When given an assignment due Friday afternoon, do the research, check the numbers, make the copies and have it on the boss's desk Thursday. Get the reputation for finishing projects early.

How many union organizing campaigns have been abandoned because someone dropped the ball, failed to return calls, lost contact, or got distracted?

308. Decide Important or Urgent

Everything we do in organizing is important. Phone calls need to be made, meetings require attendance, workers need to be visited. We need to prioritize things seen as urgent. These belong on the top of our To Do list. Anything that if not completed could end up costing your job is urgent. Assignments identified as important by our supervisors are urgent. Anything that might leave a worker in limbo is urgent. Attending your kid's soccer games, taking your spouse out on birthdays, attending a friend's funeral Double-Urgent. Don't let relationships become casualties of the labor movement.

309. Make a Banner Frame

How to Make the Perfect Banner Frame

Banners need to be pulled tight to be displayed. Having a lightweight portable frame will allow it to be set up quickly and moved from location to location easily. A good banner will grab people's attention and help get your message out to the public. You'll look like a pro because your banner will have greater visibility. This frame is designed to hold a banner in place even in mild winds.

Follow these simple instructions to make an inexpensive, easy to assemble, collapsible frame made from PVC pipe. In this example, we will assemble a frame for a banner measuring approximately 4 feet high and 12 feet in length, with a minimum of 12 grommets.

Gather the following tools and materials

- Banner with Grommets

- Marker

- Hacksaw or PVC Cutter

- Tape Measure

- Knife

- 50 ft- 1 Inch PVC Pipe

- 2- 1" PVC 90 Degree Elbows

- 6- 1" PVC "T" Connectors

- PVC "X" Connector

- 12- 6" Ball Bungees Instructions

1. Measure pipes 4–72 inch, 3–48 inch, 9–12 inch.

2. Cut the pipes to the proper lengths.

3. Clean the shavings off with a knife.

4. Lay the banner face down on ground.

5. Assemble the pieces over the banner.

6. Thread the ball bungees through the grommets.

7. Wrap the ball bungees around the pipe frame.

8. Stand the frame up and twist the feet in place.

Note: The longer pieces will run along the top and bottom of the banner. Two of the three medium-length pieces will run from top to bottom on the outside edges and one will reinforce the center. The two PVC elbows hold the top corners together. The "X" connector is for the bottom center of the frame. All the rest of the connections will be made with "T" connectors. The 9 – 12-inch pipes make up the feet to hold the banner up without having to hold it. You will not need glue to attach the pieces.

The completed frame should extend 2 inches from the edge of the banner to the inside edge of the frame. The banner should be pulled tight. One-inch PVC pipe works best. Anything less may be too flimsy. PVC Fittings allow the various pieces of pipe to be fitted together easily and disassembled when finished. The frame is reinforced in the middle to keep the frame from bending. To transport your banner frame, bundle the pipes together and wrap with ball bungees.

Congratulations on making the perfect union organizing banner frame! It is lightweight, portable, inexpensive to make, and easily assembled.

Humble Beginnings

There we were, in front of the medical center project on Westwood Plaza at the University of California Los Angeles campus. We were bringing to the public's attention a non-union contractor had received numerous non-compliance notices on the project, even a stop-work order. We were convinced students and faculty would care. We thought we might even get the media to cover us on the nightly news. Perhaps even get the contractor removed from the job. That didn't happen.

Admittedly, we were new to all this. While we were experts at picketing, hand-billing and accessing jobsites as organizers, bannering was just something we hadn't tried. There were no how-to articles or books written on the subject. We were pretty much making it up as we were going along.

As an organizer you learn a few things over the years about designing flyers; keep the text to a minimum, use bright colors to attract attention, stick with easy to read fonts.

From my experience in a band I learned a few things about banners; use large grommets, tape looks sloppy, thickness matters. Having a banner with the band name clearly presented is one way to get concert goers to remember the name of your group from the others performing on the same bill. You quickly realize that concert promoters fail to properly introduce acts and with so many bands performing in a single night people naturally forget which band they just saw. Having a banner solves the problem and helps people remember.

Our first attempt at bannering at the campus of UCLA didn't go so well. It seemed we chose the perfect location with lots of traffic. We unfurled the banner and held it in place by pulling it tight between us. After a few moments, the banner would tend to sag in the middle. To counter this, we would pull harder sometimes yanking the person on the other end. The harder one person pulled the harder the other person had to compensate. It was difficult to grip the edge of the banner without folding it over. Our arms were getting tired. We couldn't stand up straight because the other person was pulling.

Soon a slight breeze kicked up presenting another problem. Even in the lightest breeze, the banner acted like a sail. We were being pushed and pulled in all directions. No doubt we must have looked silly out there stumbling around trying to hold that banner in place. We decided then and there we needed a portable frame to hold the banner taut. We weren't sure exactly what type of material we would use for the frame, but after some discussion, we agreed on PVC pipe. A trip to Home Desperate would help us decide on the size and dimensions.

The following day we came back to the same spot with a custom-made portable banner frame and bungees to attach the banner. Now we were in business. We assembled the frame quickly and held the banner in place. Even in a slight breeze! It was easy to hold in place and if one of us positioned ourselves in the center the other could take a break or use the restroom.

The design was still not complete. It seemed a little unsteady at times, and it still required holding it in place. It seemed another pipe in the center would help to reinforce the frame. By changing some fittings out, we came up with a plan to add feet. After bannering for a few hours, we returned to the office and tweaked the design a bit. A few trips to the store and the design was nearly perfect.

The following day we were back. By now our design was nearly complete. We set up the frame and walk away for a moment and engage the public who were eager to speak with us. The frame still seemed to lean forward or backward just a few inches. No problem unless there was a breeze. That slight leaning made the frame rock back and forth which eventually allowed the wind to knock it over.

We solved this problem by adding end caps to the feet. Now the design was complete.

The next several days I bannered by myself, knowing the effort would cause a stir, but no way of knowing what effect if any it would have on the project. Eventually, I was approached by a student reporter at the Daily Bruin. He wanted more information about the project and the contractor. This led to meetings with other students.

Location-Location-Location

During one of these discussions, a student asked, "Why banner in front of the job? Why not place it in front of the chancellor's office?" Ah hah! None of us had thought of that. We thought locating the banner in front of the project made the most sense, but decisions about which contractors to use were made on a much higher level. Those people were who we needed to motivate.

We were happy to relocate because it began to feel that each day it had less and less effect. The chancellor's office was on a shady street, with parking that was more convenient, with park benches and more foot traffic.

The change of scenery did us a lot of good and the very first day the chancellor's secretary came out to talk to us. Earlier that morning the chancellor had walked by on his way back from lunch, not recognizing him, we attempted to give him a button with a similar slogan as our banner. He didn't accept it, instead, he went into his office and called a meeting of his staff to discuss the problem contractor on the hospital project.

310. Improve Your Bannering

10 Tips for Better Bannering

The goal of using a banner is to grab people's attention, even in a city where there are billboards and signs competing for every glance. It's a high-profile way for union organizers to get a message to the public. You've probably seen a labor dispute where this tactic was used. A banner might read something like, "Shame on Acme Builders/Labor Dispute." It can be very effective if done properly. Here are some tips for maximum visibility and effectiveness.

1. Keep the Headline Brief – Limit your words to seven or less. Anything more and people will lose the message.

2. Make a collapsible PVC Frame – Assemble a sturdy portable frame made from inexpensive PVC pipe.

3. Recruit Volunteers – The more volunteers the better. It sends a message to the public that real people are behind the dispute.

4. Avoid High Winds – A banner tends to act like a sail even in the slightest winds. Order a union made banner with plenty of grommets and secure it with ball bungees.

5. Pick a High Traffic Area – Set up along busy traffic routes for drivers and pedestrians to see. Get the message to as many people as you can in the shortest amount of time.

6. Choose the Right Time – Make the biggest impact by timing your activities for peak traffic and maximum visibility.

7. Hand Something Out – Distribute leaflets, stickers, or buttons. This is an opportunity to connect with the public. You could also collect signatures on a petition.

8. Turn Up the Pressure – In the beginning start out slow and each day increase the amount of time and the number of volunteers. Your mission is to create a situation that builds momentum.

9. Never Fold a Banner – Avoid leaving permanent creases and wrinkles. Gently roll-up the banner when you are finished.

10. Enjoy Yourself – Show enthusiasm for what you're doing. Your delivery is as important as the message on the banner.

311. Don't Compromise

Don't be so quick to compromise. Sometimes union organizers have a winning strategy and share their ideas, only to be shot down by others often less experienced than themselves. Just because someone tried and failed years ago, doesn't mean we should abandon all hope. Be careful not to allow naysayers to influence your actions.

312. Be Charismatic

Confidence is certainly one trait shared by charismatic people. The ability to strike up a conversation and keep it going is another. Communicating with and mirroring another's feelings is essential too. Traits union organizers often possess, are the abilities to attract people to join a cause or group. We've been told by experts to give firm handshakes and look people directly in the eyes. These nonverbal cues let others know they can trust us. We've been trained since birth to identify when motives are not genuine. Add integrity to the list of attractive qualities. All these abilities and more, are what make people charismatic.

313. Discourage Nepotism

As union organizers, we're not always consulted about decisions that affect organizations, but if given the opportunity, discourage nepotism. It's killing the labor movement.

It's hard to argue the boss's son is the best person for the job with hundreds of potential applicants available. Even if all the others were interviewed (and they never are) it isn't believable. Such practices set the administration up for criticism and the organization up for further legal and financial scrutiny. Additionally, favoritism on the job can be a suable form of employment discrimination. Few organizations can afford the liability of potential lawsuits stemming from real or perceived favoritism. The same goes for awarding contracts to close friends or relatives. Hiring family members and friends can negatively affect employee morale. The boss's son sees himself as "bullet-proof" knowing he'll never be fired or laid off. Is that the right person to have on the team?

An effective way to discourage nepotism would be for labor organizations to pass anti-nepotism bylaws. With policies in place and uniformly followed, employee morale would greatly improve.

314. Be Discreet

Union organizing campaigns require organizers to be discreet. We deal with confidential information often. The potential consequences for workers requires us to be prudent and show self-restraint when it comes to sharing information. We must be trusted to organize effectively.

315. Disconnect for a Spell

If we spend hours staring at a computer screen, television or personal device we need to disconnect for a spell. Avoid many of the problems related with always being tied to a device. Interact with family, spouse, and friends. Communication online is important, but we need to make sure the people we love the most have our undivided attention. There are many benefits to disconnecting at key times during the day such as during meals and at bedtime. First is reducing eye strain. We've all seen people squinting to see their phones and devices. Consider wearing glasses with lens coatings specially made to reduce eye strain. Hours and hours of eye strain could lead to blurred vision. Next, experience better sleep by turning off devices an hour before bedtime. This gives the body time to decompress. Another trick is to dim lights before bedtime to give our circadian clock a cue that it's getting late. Ever notice how hard it can be to go to bed early in the summertime?

316 Introduce New Ideas

Bold new ideas are needed in the labor movement. More cost-effective, efficient ways of conducting union organizing drives await our discovery. The trick to introducing new ideas is to find the right time, with tact and perseverance.

Here's a story about how not to go about it. An organizer marched into a meeting, "all guns blazing" so to speak. Frustrated with the lack of consistency in messaging between locals, she proposed hiring a marketing firm for an outside perspective. The new firm would review all materials and come up with a consistent strategy for outreach. Improved graphics and pamphlets would also be included. Most of us agreed with the findings, but not the delivery. Several in attendance were offended, others were concerned about the cost. She contacted some of us after the meeting and shared an impressive written proposal. I printed it, promising to back her up next time it was brought up. Unfortunately, she was terminated the next day.

317. Ask the Leader to Deliver Bad News

Ask the leader to deliver any bad news. This way it will be easier for followers to digest. Be appreciated, not resented.

318. Keep Talking Points Handy

Create talking points and have them ready when needed. Take a few moments to gather needed information together. Do a little research online. Often union organizers are asked to speak at public hearings and planning commission meetings. Sometimes it's before friendly supporters and other times against hostile adversaries. Either way, it's a good idea to have talking points available. Don't read from a script, but feel free to glance down at notes if stuck on a topic. Even with talking points, we may get a question we don't know the answer to. When this happens, it's a good idea to tell the person we will find out and get back to them, then follow up.

319. Organize with Student Interns

Sponsoring a student intern can be a very effective and cost-efficient way to help your organizing efforts. Many colleges offer labor studies programs in which student interns earn college credits for their efforts. These are often young, vibrant people who have a variety of skills and knowledge that you need. Consider how a student might help to do research for upcoming campaigns or create a database of workers or help contact other students or activities.

Most local unions don't even consider student interns. Perhaps it's because unions tend to recruit help from within the organizations themselves. Whatever the reason, it would be to your advantage to look further into hiring or sponsoring a student intern for organizing.

Most interns will have no knowledge of your organization or its history, but they will be eager to learn. Take time to explain the industry you are in and the challenges you face. Some student interns will have previous union organizing experience and move on to work in the labor movement.

An intern assigned to work with me helped the organization greatly. We spent a few days driving from jobsite to jobsite contacting workers and getting a feel for what organizers do. After getting acquainted and hearing about the problems unions face, he had an idea for creating an organizing brochure. Within a few days, he had completed an impressive full-color brochure, which we used from that point forward. Student interns come with a variety of skills and interests, and, if given the opportunity, they can really make a difference.

On another occasion, we created a survey designed to help gather names, addresses, phone numbers, skill level, and attitudes of workers on a construction site for an organizing campaign. I had already been on the project and gathered as much information as I could. The intern, posing as a student doing research on construction careers, could stop workers at the gate and gather the information needed. Because of his age, no one doubted for a moment that he was doing an assignment for a school project. The workers were very cooperative and gladly filled out the survey. Later he input the answers into a database and mailed a follow-up to each worker with the results of the survey. He could compare their lower nonunion wages with that of union workers and include information about the union's medical insurance and retirement plan.

The most interesting part of working with an intern was that with all the excitement of our organizing campaign, the intern was more content in performing routine research. The research was the part that always was hardest for me. Gathering information online and inputting it in a database was a part of the job I dreaded the most. He could do it in half the time that I could. Unfortunately for our organization, the internship lasted only for the summer, and soon he returned to school. It was great to have an outsider's view of our campaign to point out the things we might not notice ourselves. I'm convinced he found the experience as rewarding as we did.

320. Make Regular Appearances

There's a lot to be said for showing up on a regular basis and making yourself visible. People get to know who you are; they connect a face with the name. Over time they come to respect you and understand your cause. It can happen anywhere people come together to meet; job bids, work sites, churches, universities, school board meetings, union meetings, city council meetings, etc.

In the city of Los Angeles, there are two characters who have taken this idea of making regular appearances to an extreme. Please note: I'm not recommending you emulate their behavior. I'm only showing how making regular appearances can get you known, in some cases even famous. David "Zuma Dogg" Saltsburg and John Walsh, are arguably two of the most infamous politicians in the city of Los Angeles. They appear on television weekly grilling city leaders with pointed questions. They are on a first name basis with most politicians in Los Angeles including the mayor. Both get invited and attend numerous parties and functions. The news media seek their comments. Despite all this, neither has a snowball chance in hell of ever being elected to public office. These individuals are what's commonly referred to as "social gadflies." They have a legal right to speak at city council meetings just as any other citizen. The difference is, they have made careers speaking on almost "every issue," whenever and wherever the city has a public hearing. Zuma Dogg often wears clothes with his name prominently displayed on them. He's appeared on the Howard Stern Show and was interviewed by Larry King. John Walsh flails his arms around while he talks. He ends most comments by plugging his website, HollywoodHighlands dot org or his blog JWalshconfidential. All this is aired daily on television in a city that loves good entertainment.

If you attended a job bid, worksite, church, university, school board meeting, union meeting, city council meeting in your town, would anyone recognize you? If not, perhaps you should begin making regular appearances.

321. Show You Trust Them

Workers put their trust in our competence and our ability. We demonstrate trust to workers by empowering them to lead their fellow coworkers to victory. Put them in charge of the campaign. Step back and let the workers organize themselves, under the direction and guidance of the union.

322. Practice Making Quick Decisions

When we get comfortable making quick small decisions it makes making bigger decisions easier. There are dozens of decisions needed to see a union organizing campaign to completion. Stalling for days to weigh the pros and cons will only hurt the group's efforts. There are potential stalling points from the initial phone call to the union from an interested party, to who will be the designated union observer on election day. Don't get bogged down in minor details or leave people hanging. Practice making quick decisions.

When receiving an initial phone call from a group of workers interested in organizing their workplace, don't hang the phone up without setting a time, date and location for a meeting. If the first time isn't convenient, recommend another. The point is not to leave the group hanging. Pick a time, date and location quickly.

In high school, I worked in the fast food industry. A bus would pull up full of hungry customers. They'd pack the lobby shoulder to shoulder in line while we scrambled to take their orders. After waiting-in-line for ten minutes or so grown adults would get to the register and only then look up at the menu. "Hmmm, let me see" they would pause. "No, I had a cheeseburger last week" reading the menu. Sometimes they would wait till the last minute, look down at their four-year-old child and say, "Jimmy, what would you like?" Inevitably the kid who couldn't read and barely knew where he was would say something like, "macaroni and cheese," which wasn't on the menu. Then the adult would read the menu aloud to the kid skipping coffee of course. We wanted to pull our hair out.

323. Conduct an Organizing Conference

19 Tips for Organizing Conference Planners

Feeling overwhelmed with responsibility in planning your union's organizing conference? Where do you start? What needs to be included? What if anything should be done differently this time?

It's no easy task. You must choose the right location, the right venue, and it needs to run like a well-oiled machine. You want to send people home feeling refreshed and ready with new tools to do their job better.

Here are 19 tips to help you conduct a successful organizing conference everyone will enjoy.

1. Review Objective – Ask "Why an organizing conference?" then set a goal and work toward it.

2. Plan for Fun – Host it at a location people enjoy and give them time to enjoy it.

3. Keep it short – Two or three days max; don't take your best people out-of-the-field for too long.

4. Build Them Up – It's easy to get discouraged as an organizer. Encourage attendee's success.

5. Limit Teleprompters – Good leaders make accomplished speakers. Teleprompters distract.

6. Skip the Entertainment – Organizing is a fascinating topic. Keep the focus on organizing.

7. Limit Speakers to 15 Minutes – Less if possible. Everyone will thank you!

8. Remind People to Bring a Sweater – Conference rooms are often chilly.

9. Keep it light – Organizers are the most overworked people in the labor movement.

10. Give Them a Break – Regular restroom breaks lead to better attention and retention.

11. Limit Evening Receptions – After a long day glued to a chair most would rather pass.

12. Repeat Theme Often – Ask each speaker to include a reference so it's not forgotten.

13. Start and End on Time – Be respectful of attendee's time and travel arrangements.

14. Have Contingency Plans – Be ready if a speaker fails to show or computer malfunctions.

15. Keep It Relevant – If the subject is anything but better organizing it should be dropped.

16. Don't Preach to the Choir – Organizers know exactly why they do what they do.

17. Limit Who Attends – Raise the bar by requiring attendees be full-time union organizers.

18. Discover New Talent – Bring in new people to conduct seminars and breakout sessions.

19. End Strong – As participants depart they should feel relaxed, motivated, and energized.

Having attended dozens of organizing conferences by various unions, it's obviously challenging to meet people's expectations. Some speakers are dry-as-a-bone and others get way off topic. At one such event an entertainer juggled bowling-balls. While it was entertaining, many in the audience were confused. What does that have to do with organizing? Each conference goer has their own taste in music, food, format and venue. By following these 19 tips, you can rest assured your union's organizing conference will remain focused on "union organizing." Participants will leave informed and ready to take on the job ahead.

324. Accept Criticism

Criticism sucks! Sometimes it's unwarranted, and other times it strikes with pinpoint accuracy. The truth can feel like a punch to the kidney. We need to think of it as feedback, own it, adjust our sails, and journey on.

Accepting criticism isn't something that comes easily for me. It's been a recurring problem in my life. Once, I asked a favor of an early mentor, someone I deeply respect and admire. He had every intention of helping me the following week. I failed to remind him as asked. Later that week, instead of admitting I blew it by not reminding him, I called him out in a meeting in front of all our colleagues. He owned it, apologized publicly, and continued with his report. Toward the end he said something that took a week to realize was intended at me, he said, "at least I admit when I'm wrong."

When I got laid off at the Mobile Refinery in Torrance, CA a coworker said I had been "floundering out there" as a foreman. Ouch! That hurt. He was right though. My mind was somewhere else at the time. I didn't think anybody noticed.

325. Hand the Media a Story

Reporters need juicy stories to write about. Protestors need the attention of the public. Hand these so-called "journalists" some red-meat and you can have all the free advertising you could ever want.

That's what my friend, visual effects artist Dave Rand did at the 2013 Oscar's in Hollywood. VFX artists were planning a protest to bring attention to the plight of workers after the closure of the company behind the movie Life of Pi. Unfortunately, the Hollywood police department restricted protestors to a small area blocks away from the red-carpet. There were 450 VFX artists protesting. Things seemed hopeless because of the distance to the event. Reporters were ignoring the protests until Dave chartered a small plane to circle above the ceremony pulling a banner protesting the treatment of VFX artists. Suddenly the news media were everywhere. During an acceptance speech, the academy cut-the-mic of one of the recipients who attempted to bring attention to the protests. That only added to the story.

326. Expose Paid Protestors

Private companies such as crowdsondemand.com and others offer paid protestors and "concerned citizens" for a variety of uses by businesses. These are usually low-paid actors willing to do just about anything for a buck; even speaking in front of city councils.

327. Keep Tradition Alive

There are things we do in the labor movement to spur solidarity and camaraderie. These things are important. We need to pass them on to the next generation of workers to build a solid foundation that will last. Every local union has something they do traditionally.

In my home local, in Los Angeles, it's tradition that the business agent provides doughnuts in the hall on Friday for out of work brothers and sisters. It's a small gesture that gives those in the hall something to look forward to. Those on the out-of-work list need hope and encouragement especially heading into the weekend. What might be a prospect of rest and relaxation for someone who's employed might mean two more days without needed income to someone out of work. There are times in every person's career, where that tradition means a lot. Luckily, business agents over the years have kept the tradition alive.

There was a journeyman who bought me lunch on Fridays when I was his apprentice. Every Thursday he would remind me not to bring a lunch the next day. It became kind of an event every week. We had some great meals together. While we were only assigned to work together a short time we became good friends. Years later that was the memory we would always refer to when reminiscing about the good old days. Other journeymen on the same jobsite didn't buy their apprentices meals. It was a tradition this particular journeyman had experienced himself years earlier. He saw the value in it and passed it down. It was a tradition worthy of reciprocating and you can believe me it has been on several occasions.

Growing up we had a family friend named Ray Gregory. He was larger than life character who always wore colorful Hawaiian shirts. Ray survived the Korean war, lost his wife to cancer, had his pension pilfered and was maimed in an industrial accident. Despite all these tragedies, Ray remained one of the funniest guys to be around. His colorful Hawaiian shirts became his signature. Years later while working at the airport, the foreman reminded the group that the next day was, "Hawaiian Shirt Friday." I could hardly wait. It reminded me of good times when despite everything Ray made the simplest things fun. We all showed up the next day wearing loud floral shirts. Mine was hideous! With our hardhats and tool-belts on, we must have looked silly, but it was fun. The message it sent to the employer and anyone else who saw us working was the week's almost over. We're gonna party this weekend! It's a tradition in district 3. Who knows who started it? You don't mess with tradition.

Before being accepted into the union, my Dad convinced me to run an ad in the paper seeking experience as an electrician's helper. Within days Empire Electric in Los Angeles hired me. It was a good gig and we were treated better than we deserved. We hustled from one job to the next putting out fires. The owner Clinton Riggins was a great guy. He grew up poor and managed to make a good life for himself and his family. Clinton called me just before Thanksgiving. He wanted to know how many people mom was having over for dinner. Later, he called again asking to meet him in a parking lot of a supermarket. There he handed me the biggest frozen turkey he could find. He said it was tradition to give all his employees a turkey at Thanksgiving. My mother was so proud of me bringing home that turkey. It barely fit in the oven. That was a great Thanksgiving feast! His gesture was the subject of many conversations over the years. Mom would ask how my old boss was doing, but we had fallen out of touch. After joining the union and graduating from the apprenticeship Clinton's stepson ended up on the same jobsite. We had worked together at Empire Electric. He had also joined the union since then. Clinton had passed away by this time. We both talked fondly of him. Clinton was a great guy. He will always be remembered.

328. Designate an Organizing Bulletin Board

Put an organizing bulletin board in the hall and include photos of members volunteering and participating in union activities. Update it regularly and include as many people as possible. Add the word "Organize" or "Organizing" on top.

There was a finished aluminum bulletin board stored in the high bay. It was the type you could lock. We put it up in the hall and soon it became the organizing bulletin board. In the summer, we displayed photos of members volunteering at the local picnic. During the holidays, the photos from the Christmas Party were a hit. In between, we filled the board with pictures of pickets, hearings, members applying at non-union shops, apprentice skill competition, etc. The active members loved seeing themselves and those that were less active had a chance to see what they were missing. It became a great tool for informing everyone about organizing.

After giving a monthly report at the union meeting we often referred attendees to the bulletin board. They would congregate in front of it looking to see if they recognized their friends. It was a great tool. On more than one occasion, the business manager was seen admiring the pictures.

A few years after leaving the position, I dropped by the hall to catch up with friends at the Annual Christmas Party. To my surprise, the organizing bulletin board still had the same photos up. I took that as a sign...

329. Retire in Your Prime

Don't become a dinosaur. Retire with enough energy to travel and pursue other interests.

Some years ago, a hard-working and very industrious union member was preparing to retire. He and his wife were doing very well. They sold their home in the city and moved to their cabin in the mountains near Big Bear Lake. There they intended to spend their golden years together enjoying the slower paced mountain lifestyle. To hear him describe the neighborhood you could tell he had done his homework to find such an idyllic place. A new administration came into office around this time needing help. He put off retirement for a spell to assist the fledgling group. His wife occupied the cabin, while he stayed behind, hold up in a cheap hotel in the city. Time passed and before he knew it his wife became ill and died all alone. After that, he immersed himself in his work. Friends begged him to retire. Though he was well-off, he lived simply and drove an ugly station wagon. Eventually, he became ill and died. At his funeral, one person after another got up to speak about how much he had helped them. While many of us were in awe of his service to the members, we wished he had taken time to retire and enjoy life. We couldn't help but feel he worked all those years and never really lived.

330. Attend Memorial Services

Be there for members and staff when they need you most. They will appreciate your presence.

Just a week after being hired as a union organizer a staff member's mother passed away suddenly. It was a solemn service. We were there to pay our respects, each dressed in black. A few days later a long-time member died. The business agent was not available. I was asked to attend the service and deliver a Bible to the family. Someone had already confirmed the religion of the member. The service was anything but traditional. There was music and food and the whole thing lasted no more than 30 minutes. The person leading the memorial mentioned the body had been cremated so we wouldn't be going to a gravesite. I met the family and gave them the keepsake Bible provided by the union. It was enclosed in a beautiful wooden box. They appreciated the gesture. The deceased's sister spoke fondly of her brother, his love of woodworking and how he was a proud union member. "He's here you know," she pointed across the room. I walked over to the area where she pointed. There sitting on a table was a hand-made gourd cremation urn the member made in anticipation of his own death. It was a beautiful service which apparently went exactly as planned.

A few years later, my mother went to be with the Lord. Several staff members attended the funeral Mass. Afterwards, there was a reception with food and drinks. It felt good to have the support of my coworkers and other members who took the time out of their busy schedules to be there for the family. We were hurting. Mom was the center of our universe. Things would never be the same again.

After the reception, we joined the procession that drove across the valley arriving at San Fernando Mission Cemetery. Most of the cars peeled away at various points along the route. It was after all a workday. We needed one more pallbearer to lift Mom's casket from the hearse to her final resting place. Just then, a staff member arrived who wasn't available to attend the earlier service. He saw our predicament and offered to help. I will always be grateful for him being there in our time of need. He was respectful and dignified and a true friend.

331. Avoid Fidgeting

Exude confidence by not giving cues that seem to say you are nervous, bored or insecure. Excessive hand-wringing, foot tapping, and other forms of restlessness are signals of inattention.

332. Anticipate Future Challenges

Keep an eye out for potential organizing challenges. These may include legislation, industry trends, nonunion competition, and other unions stealing work. No industry stays the same. Unions who don't pay attention to future challenges find themselves being edged-out, merged or bankrupt.

333. Hire Slowly Fire Quickly

There are good reasons to be cautious when hiring. One wrong person in a position of influence can cause considerable liability as well as hurt morale. It's why we need to take our time bringing people onboard. Conversely, when things aren't working out it's best to cut people loose quickly without a lot of drama.

334. Invest in Professional Headshots

Find an aspiring photographer or invest in professional headshots. Get some feedback on which photos to use. The best headshots are proportional with eyes at one third. You will need both color and black and white, depending on the circumstance.

335. Contact Suppliers and Vendors

Suppliers and vendors know who the players are in any industry. Reach out to these contacts for information. Find out where the work is being done and by whom. Ask them to refer candidates and potential members.

336. Make Better House Calls

Visiting workers in their homes away from the workplace is a proven way to attract new members and support for a union. House calls disarm employers and empower workers. In the safety of their own home, workers are free to explore opportunities and ask questions that they might not feel comfortable asking in front of their co-workers or supervisor. House calling is by far the most fun and effective way to get the message to workers. Follow these guidelines to make the greatest impact:

- Be professional

- Do not intimidate

- Dress appropriately

- Don't sell – listen

- House call before dark

- Remember, safety first

- Watch for dogs

- Pair up volunteers with organizers

At the home of a nonunion worker, a funny thing happens. The employer loses all control over "its" employee. Compare this with the grip employers enjoy over employees at work, and it's as if the company was based in another country altogether. Although not everyone agrees, I think house calls are a lot of fun. In fact, there have been members who volunteered to do house calls only to chicken out at the last minute. Yet there are union members who are eager to help spread the word, and it's satisfying to know that we can rely on their help.

It's normal to get butterflies in your stomach, especially on the first house call. There's always a concern that a dog might attack, or someone might be having a particularly bad day, but most often things work out just fine. That's not to say you won't experience some unpleasant visits. If it wasn't for these visits, everyone would want to participate.

337. Do Some Pre-Meeting Coordination

Let's say we are hosting a town-hall meeting, or a meeting open to workers from the night shift. We want the meeting to run smoothly without it being interrupted or hijacked by management plants. To do this we need some pre-meeting coordination to assign roles and review the agenda. Staff and volunteer organizing committee members need to know who is in charge. Who will do introductions? Who will be speaking? How will questions be taken? What issues are important to discuss? How long will the meeting last? What is the plan if things get heated? What stories might help people relate to why the union is so important? A pre-meeting can help improve the odds of a successful outcome.

338. Keep Your Vehicle Clean

First impressions are important. Roll up like a boss. Wash your vehicle, vacuum the carpets and trunk, and shine up the tires. Air out your car before picking up passengers.

An often-overlooked maintenance item on late model cars is changing the cabin air filter. These should be replaced at regular intervals to avoid bad odors from the air conditioner and heater.

339. Upgrade Your Equipment

Upgrade equipment long before it becomes obsolete. Some organizations run so lean, upgrades become nearly impossible. Equipment is often easier to replace when it's working than broken.

340. Don't Rush the Cards

Avoid the most common mistake made by rookie and veteran organizers alike. Don't rush the process of gathering representation cards. Here is how it typically happens; a unit of workers approaches a union wanting representation. The organizer schedules a meeting with the workers and soon discovers the group has a rudimentary understanding of the NLRB process. The employees are in a rush, highly motivated and ready to sign cards. They are confident they can persuade the remaining coworkers (who didn't attend the meeting) to also sign cards.

The organizer asks everyone at the first meeting to sign cards, all agree. Soon the VOC members are gathering additional cards from their coworkers at work. Cards start trickling in, a few at first then more and more. Somewhere along the process, you find out the unit is larger than first expected. "Oh, those must be the 10 new hires we've been hearing about," someone says. You update your employee list accordingly.

Now even more cards are needed. The VOC tries to reach out to the new workers. Word gets back to management. Supervisors start asking around to find out, "who's been talking with the union?" Management holds a captive audience meeting to discuss unions. Soon people aren't willing to sign cards and the process starts to lose momentum. The remaining VOC members start to get anxious. The pressure they feel at work is palpable. They are sure they have been identified by management.

If something isn't done soon they might lose their jobs. They start skipping follow up meetings scheduled by the organizer or threaten to abandon the organizing effort all-together. The organizer or business manager hastily decides to file the RC Petition. There are enough cards to legally file but far less than the needed amount to insure a comfortable victory. He or she resolves to make up for the lack of cards by throwing resources toward the effort during the last weeks of the campaign. Extra people will be assigned to do house calls, honk-and-waves, rallies, just days before the vote. T-shirts are printed up, signs are made, meanwhile, the VOC is reporting strong support. Feedback from recent house calls shows only lukewarm support. Some supporters will be out-of-town the day of the vote. On election day, the group comes up short by a hand-full of votes. How could this happen? Simple, the organizer rushed the cards.

Take your time. Work methodically to acquire no less than 70% of cards for a given unit. Beware, management often prevails in adding workers to the bargaining unit thereby diluting your support. Listen carefully to your VOC but take their assessments with a grain of salt.

341. Interview More People Than the Last Organizer

Want results? Outwork everyone else. Roll up your sleeves and get busy. Always be meeting with potential members. Walk more jobsites. Double book appointments if needed.

Become proficient at gathering the required documents and information. Put paperwork in order so the next person doesn't have to second guess your work. Streamline processes so they become second nature.

Early in my career, many candidates who took the time to schedule a meeting failed to show. To combat the problem appointments were followed up with email reminders, phone calls, and postcards. You've probably experienced a similar process when you set up a doctor visit. We double and triple booked candidates. The process worked so well, it became a necessity to have one candidate filling out an information form in the day room while another was in the office interviewing. We had a stack of clipboards with information sheets and a pen attached. If someone walked-in off the street they were seen too.

The good thing about having a process is soon everyone will know the drill. Say you are across town and running late, your secretary or coworker can get the process started in your absence. "Here, fill this out. The organizer will be in shortly." Problem solved. Have more one-on-one conversations and interactions than the last organizer to increase your odds of success.

342. Make it Personal

Tell stories. Allow people to get to know who you are. Connect with people on a personal level. Give them details in your presentations and conversations. Let them know about your love of classic cars or the fish that got away on your camping trip, how you got started in your career and perhaps more importantly, why you think the person is well suited to succeed in your union. It's those little details we learn about each other that allow for authentic personal communication. Where are you coming from? What makes you unique? What similarities do we share with each other? These are the details that allow people to relate to one another.

Some friends dropped by to see the neighborhood and check out the house. They brought a coworker along who was interested in foreclosures. He heard my story and wanted to see if he could find a similar deal. A divorced couple had owned the home but fell behind on their payments. They did all kinds of renovations prior to the bank repossessing the property. It sat vacant for a year! Finally, the bank let it go for a fraction of what the previous owners paid. It was a steal! There were two others at the same price.

Back at the house, he noticed a display cabinet that held my vintage glass-grapes collection. You know, the mid-century kitsch popular in the 1960's and 70's? Glass grapes are made of Lucite, not glass and are sometimes attached to driftwood. They remind me of my childhood. Years later, he comes across some glass-grapes while cleaning out a deceased relatives home. Imagine my surprise, when a package arrived with the most beautiful glass-grapes inside. A note was enclosed saying he wanted them to go to a good home.

Go ahead, make it personal. Share some details about yourself. Connect with people on a personal level.

343. Add Accessories

Look sharp and stand out in a crowd by adding a few stylish accessories. Add a hero piece; cufflinks, pocket square, tie clip, watch, to make an ordinary suit pop. For a cocktail dress add; earrings, necklace, belt, small purse or coat.

Leave the huge overstuffed wallet at home. It looks like you are trying to sneak a double burger in your pocket. Choose a thin billfold and carry only the essentials.

344. Use Keywords and Phrases

When posting online choose industry related keywords and phrases to be found in searches. People often research topics before making important decisions. Help workers find you by including words that describe your union and the services you provide. Keywords and phrases make it easy to be discovered.

345. Look for the Underserved

Who is most underserved in your industry? There you will likely find workers who need union representation. They are on the fringe; underpaid, working long hours, unsafe conditions, experiencing wage theft, being taken advantage of. Some examples of the underserved might be; pot store workers, strippers, freelancers/1099ers, independent contractors, unclassified workers, day laborers, etc.

346. Vote the Slate

Vote for politicians with a proven track record of supporting working people. Make the list or "union slate" available for members. Place it in the union hall. Mail it to member's homes. Deliver it to worksites. Often local's wait to mail the union slate the week of the election, but many members vote via absentee ballot, so mail it early.

347. Meet the Labor Cops

Some police departments have "labor cops" who deal with unions, pickets, and other labor-related issues. Labor cops are more common in big cities. They tend to dress in plain clothes as opposed to uniforms and drive unmarked cars. These officers provide a valuable service. They are well versed in labor laws as well as police regulations. Their purpose is to help alleviate labor unrest and counsel regular police officers who are unaware union organizing is a federally protected activity.

It's a good idea to meet with these officers on a regular basis to establish rapport. Exchange business cards. Once we get to know them and they become familiar with us, we'll feel more comfortable notifying them before putting up a picket or protest. They will appreciate that we kept them informed and acted professionally. This can be very helpful. They might recommend a different approach when picketing or intervene on our behalf with a property owner that is not giving us access to workers.

On one project, a general contractor considered making a citizen's arrest of organizers for trespassing. The labor cops advised him not to because it would lead to expensive litigation and was likely a bad arrest. The general contractor considered the advice and decided to allow the organizers access to the jobsite during the worker's lunch break.

Often when informed of a situation in advance, labor cops will show up to observe. Use the opportunity to reintroduce yourself and swap business cards. A well-informed labor cop can be useful when dealing with security guards.

348. Hold an Open House

Hold an open house to attract new members and employers to your union. It requires a commitment of time. You'll need to make yourself available to gather information and show people around. Maybe you have a training facility you want to highlight or increase visibility of your local union hall, reach out to government contractors, or identify workers on government contracts, regardless of the reason holding an open house can help you accomplish your goal.

Having an open house, for example, the second Tuesday of every month at 6 pm, is likely to be more successful than just a one-off. Maybe the person you invite is busy this month but could make it next time. If you have the event on a regular basis you could use the same flyer over and over. People will be more likely to refer friends by word-of-mouth if you have the event on a repeat schedule.

There are things to consider when planning an open house. How will it be advertised? Will food be served? Will it be a small or a large event? How much help will be needed? Should there be a program with speakers or just a tour of the facility? For large events consider hiring a caterer. If it's a morning event donut and coffee might be sufficient. Later in the day, you might want to have pizzas available or a barbeque. Some local unions have amazing barbeque trailers that could be utilized for such an event. It depends on the number of people expected to attend and the budget. Make sure any area where food is served is clean and tidy. Consider having staff wear similar color shirts so attendees know who to approach with questions.

349. Organize Service Contract Work

Locate government contracts by searching on
www.fedbizopps.gov . Search by contract number, zip code, federal
agency, classification, set-asides, awarded contracts, existing work,
etc. Service Contract Act falls under the NLRB.

350. Request Documents

The Labor Board is good at compelling employers to provide
documents when the request is reasonable and sensible.
Remember; documents don't lie. Request documents to strengthen
your case.

351. Know Your Mandatory Bargaining Subjects

Wages, hours and working conditions are mandatory bargaining
subjects. Know the difference between permissive and illegal
subjects of bargaining.

352. Make Your Message Clear

Be sure everyone on your team is on the same page. It's frustrating
when leaders give mixed messages. Avoid giving a five-minute
speech and assuming everyone understands the main points. Break
the message down so people understand, "This month we are
fighting for ......" fill in the blank. Stick with tangibles such as
policy changes or things you have the power to change.

A woman handed me a flyer. There was type front and back around
10 paragraphs total. "What's the issue," I asked? She went into a
long explanation about grocery workers being mistreated. "That's
your headline," I said. "Grocery Workers Mistreated."

A common mistake people make when designing a leaflet is
forgetting to include a headline. Most people will only give a leaflet
a brief glance before putting it in the trash. The same goes for
signs. One quick glance and they are on their way. You need to have
a headline that sums it all up. A page full of text, no matter how

well written, is likely to be thrown into the trash without a second thought. You should be able to describe the problem in seven words or less, preferably less. You only get one chance to grab the reader's attention, so do it. Make the headline just that, a headline, just like in the newspaper. It doesn't have to describe everything, but it must demand attention.

A headline with too many words will not get read, and one with too much information will lack intensity. A great headline should push the reader's buttons, create a sense of urgency, and compel one to act.

353. Take Up a Collection

Have a worker ask permission of a low-level manager to take up a collection for new equipment. Use a piggy bank with a sign (i.e.: "Collection for tools" or "Collection for safety harnesses"). Put management on the spot for being cheap.

354. Build Instant Rapport

There are simple things you can do to build instant rapport with people you meet. Learn to validate people, be less threatening and make everyone feel more comfortable around you. Study how you interact with people. Make a conscious effort to improve your skills in this area and it will pay off in every aspect of your work and home life.

3 Phone Call Exercises for Union Organizers Who Want to Build Instant Rapport

Have you ever noticed how easy it is to tell if a person is excited to speak with you on the phone? Even without the benefit of body language 9 out of 10 times, you can tell if the person on the other end is smiling or not. Now you can use that knowledge for your own benefit when speaking with contractors and candidates on the phone. Try these 3 simple exercises to help connect and create instant rapport in 60 seconds or less.

Exercise 1: Smile when answering the phone.

Try it and see if it makes a difference. Having read about this technique a friend decided to give it a try. People immediately noticed the change and complimented her on having an uplifting attitude. It's especially good for deflecting negative energy when making cold calls. You'll find you will be less affected by frustrated callers and you might even cheer people up.

Exercise 2: Use the person's name.

People love to hear their name because it demonstrates that you are listening and personalizes the conversation. It shows a certain amount of respect and admiration and shows that you have above average people skills. Go ahead; use the person's name during a phone call.

Exercise 3: Tell the person you are glad they called.

Let the other person know how much you appreciate what they did whether they took your call or called you back. Little things make a big difference. If you don't say it, they may never know. There's no need to go overboard, just remind the person you care.

Working the phones is like delivering any professional business presentation. It takes practice to master the techniques needed to gain instant rapport. The more you do it the more comfortable you will become. Soon you will be making great first impressions, connecting on a whole new level with members and candidates alike. Add these exercises to your routine and you should see results within a few days.

355. Don't Mail Cards

The response rate of mailed cards being signed and returned is somewhere in the low teens at best. Mailing representation cards de-values their importance in the campaign. You're looking for a commitment from workers. When the individual signs an authorization card they should be encouraged not only to step-up and support the effort but ultimately to vote in-favor of the union. This requires a face-to-face conversation. It can be done by a paid organizer, but it would be more effective if done by a coworker familiar with the person. Another problem with mailing cards is they are often not properly filled out, signed and dated correctly.

A mass mailing of cards is likely to tip-off management. Even a more targeted mailing of cards can have unintended consequences. A campaign got off to a bad start when the business manager mailed cards to the previous year's supporters. Organizers lost the previous organizing drive by just a few worker's votes. The loss had a dramatic effect in the workplace. Many supporters of the previous organizing drive quit. Others who remained vowed to never go through such a bitter experience again. When word of the mailing was received by management, the company ramped up their anti-union campaign. Management focused their union avoidance efforts at the new-hires and it worked.

356. Have Members Serve on an Organizing Committee

Encourage your members to get more involved with their union by starting an internal organizing committee. This will be a group of volunteers you can count on to support your efforts.

What's in It for Them?

Serving on a volunteer organizing committee is a great way to gain experience organizing. Organizers need help finding people to assist with certain activities. Here is a list of activities members can help with:

- Picketing

- Bannering

- Leafleting

- Phone Banking

- Letter Writing

- Petitioning

- Voter Registration

A volunteer organizing committee can be a vital resource when staff finds themselves overwhelmed with assignments. The key to success as a volunteer is to participate on a consistent basis. Doing so proves a person is interested in advancing the cause of the organization. Enthusiasm shows a person is willing to go the extra mile no matter how mundane or tedious the assignment.

Getting Noticed

Becoming more involved in the union will not only strengthen the organization but will greatly improve an individual's experience as a member. As they say, "people get only what they put into it." Find ways to add value to the organization and network with key individuals who are always contributing.

Many people will rise to the occasion when asked to volunteer at an event." What is especially appreciated is someone volunteering without being asked. Even greater is a person who is flexible enough to take orders when volunteering. Be the person who steps up to solve problems.

It is less risky to recruit a person for an organizing position if the person is already an active member then it would be to take a chance on someone with no history of participation. There's the fear of the unknown. Not everyone knows how to jump in and get busy. This will be a concern of the person in charge of making hiring decisions. You can help put this person at ease by gaining a reputation as being someone who can be counted on to show up on time and doing what is needed to be done. You can convince that person of your worth by going the extra mile past what is expected of you. This will always be appreciated.

There are a variety of opportunities and activities available for one to participate in with a union. Here is a short list:

- Apprenticeship Committee

- Executive Board

- Contract Negotiating Committee

- Examining Board

- Organizing Committee

- Health and Welfare Committee

- Mentoring

- Tutoring

- Salting

- Apprentice Instructing

- Convention Delegate

- Jobsite Delegate

- Shop Steward

357. Offer Career Counseling

Working with a career counselor can save workers a great deal of time and money. Offer career counseling to people by providing information and resources that can help them find a job in the industry that interests them. Most trade schools, colleges, and universities offer free counseling through community organizations like your union.

Counselors accumulate contacts by attending job fairs, conferences, and conventions. They stay in touch with successful people. They can tune up a person's resume, warn about dangers to avoid, keep people focused on qualities that matter to employers, and help find them work or other financial opportunities that they may not have considered on their own.

Good counselors keep in touch with people in their field to help their client's get results. If you can't help them maybe you know someone who can. You can be a great resource for placing "trouble cases," such as people who have run through a string of jobs in a short period of time or have recently been released from prison.

I once took a high school placement test designed to help people find their "perfect job." It came back with something like "fertilizer engineer." I chose a different path, and I'm glad I did!

Successful people aren't always the brightest or most talented. Sometimes it's just a matter of being first or starting earlier than the next person. Getting a jump on the competition can help a person leave other applicants behind. If you can help workers find their first job, especially if it's one in the field they are most interested in, you'll be helping move them in the direction of their goal and getting valuable experience that will pay-off for them in the long run.

That's not to say that a different type of job won't help them get ahead. My first job was at a gas station. I didn't last long because I had a terrible attitude. Eventually, I was hired at a fast-food restaurant. That may not sound very glamorous (and it wasn't) but it was a valuable experience for me because I got some much-needed training in customer service. When you work in an atmosphere where "the customer is always right" you gain a real appreciation for service. It was a humbling experience, but I wouldn't trade it for anything. I learned about going the extra mile, teamwork, and the importance of having systems for regular tasks. These skills were a big help to me as I moved on to bigger and better things.

Industry specific career counseling could be just the thing to kick start your union organizing.

358. Contest Job Bids

Despite all of Labor's efforts, there are key contracts where union contractors are simply outbid. It may be the matter of a contractor needing to sharpen the pencil a bit or another contractor being more comfortable with a slim margin and the promise of expensive add-ons. However, there may be other occasions when a contractor with poor record underbids all other competitors by such a huge amount that it becomes obvious that something is just not right. Questions arise regarding substitutions of materials, crew makeup, and personnel availability. It is at times like these when you might ask yourself, "Is this contract worth trying to get rebid?" The answer will likely depend on several things, such as:

- Is it a private or public project?

- Who is the customer or awarding agency?

- What relationships do you have with key decision makers?

- What is the reputation of the contractor in question?

Answer these questions as best you can. Trying to get a contract rebid or a contractor disqualified is an uphill battle, but it can be worth the work in the end. If you feel you have a reasonable expectation of succeeding in getting the bid thrown out and decide to proceed, there are a few steps to take to reach your goal. The following is a list of ideas to help keep you on track:

- Acquire bid specifications

- Request bid documents

- Compare bid documentation to specifications

- Research listed subcontractors and suppliers

- Set up meetings with key decision makers

- Provide your findings to key decision makers

- Write a letter demanding the project be rebid

- Speak against awarding of the bid at public meetings

- Show up at events with community stakeholders

When requesting bid specifications and documentation, be advised that it may take weeks for an agency to respond to a formal written request. Because time is of the essence, you may be better off approaching affected contractors, project engineers, or sympathetic decision makers. Often bid documentation can be received as an email attachment and printed on your own, so there will be no additional cost to the person supplying the information. Keep in mind that anything you submit as part of a bid will likely be viewed by the contractor in question. An effort will be made to refute your assertions either by the contractor or the awarding agency. It's a good idea to withhold some of your arguments until the final meeting; otherwise, the opposition will be prepared to thwart all your arguments. Once a contract is awarded, people tend to circle-the-wagons to move work forward. If however, you provide a compelling enough argument, you can get projects rebid and offending contractors disqualified from bidding.

359. Speak at Public Hearings

Speaking at public hearings requires different etiquette than we might use at other times. For one thing, we'll be facing the board members and likely have our back to the audience. What we say may be broadcast on television or radio and a transcript will be made, so our words need to be chosen very carefully. We may be speaking simply to get our support or opposition on record. Therefore, it may be a good idea to read a statement to stay on topic. Conversely, we may be speaking on a topic that we feel passionate about. When it's personal, we'll only need a few talking points to stay on topic.

Here's a list of do's and don'ts of speaking at public hearings:

- Do get a copy of the agenda

- Do dress conservatively

- Do bring community stakeholders

- Do turn in a "Request to Speak" card

- Do use an address closest to the affected area

- Do show proper respect to all the speakers

- Don't go over the allotted time

- Don't engage in cross-talk with the audience

- Don't raise your voice or get carried away

- Don't come unprepared

Some meetings will incorporate a light to indicate the speaker's time is up. Three minutes is usually enough time to get a point across. Choose a specific item to speak on. If the topic is not found on the agenda, speak on a loosely related topic. In many cases, this will be tolerated if brief and to the point. Like anything, practice makes perfect. Take the opportunity to speak at the next public hearing and enjoy the process.

360. Promote Spec Language

A forward-thinking technique adopted by unions in the construction industry is the creation of safety language, also known as spec language. Agencies desperately needed to stem the tide of unqualified workers being injured on public works projects. They were concerned for the workers and the public and trying to avoid costly workers' compensation claims and injury lawsuits. Another motivator was negative publicity created when a worker perishes on the job.

Organizers created specific safety language that when inserted into a public works contract offered a solution to help stem the tide of accidents. The new language, if adopted, would require a certain ratio of graduates from approved apprenticeship programs to the number of registered apprentices. In this way, the agency could be confident that apprentices received adequate safety training and would be working under the direction of a qualified journeyman.

Spec language caused trepidation for nonunion contractors because for years' nonunion apprenticeship programs had miserable graduation rates when compared with union apprenticeship programs. The nonunion employers would have a hard time staffing their projects.

Opposition to spec language by nonunion entities has grown. They cite their contractor's inability to bid certain projects and argue that high safety standards give unions an unfair advantage. They claim that it somehow increases the overall cost of the project, but never mention the savings in reduced accidents and workers' compensation lawsuits. Anytime the opposition argues for lower safety standards, the union comes out on top.

361. Specialize in Salting

A Salt is a euphemism for a union member applying or working at a nonunion shop for organizing purposes. Salting can be done either "overtly" or "covertly," depending on the situation. The purpose for the use of salts in most cases is to organize the workers and expose the company's violations of the National Labor Relations Act or wage and hour violations. Like any tool, it needs to be used by someone who is properly trained to use it. Your union probably offers training for anyone willing to take on this responsibility, and it's recommended that you and your volunteer participate in the class.

The effect that a coworker has in being able to communicate better with a fellow employee as opposed to an organizer who may be viewed as an outsider is tremendous. Make sure the person volunteering to salt is dedicated enough to stay employed until no longer needed. The longer a salt is employed, the better the odds are of gaining coworkers' trust. It's how most unions were started in the first place, which is why salting is so effective. Companies fear the idea of workers being empowered and educated about their employee rights.

When applying for work overtly, the applicant makes no effort to hide union affiliation. Former union companies that the applicant has worked for might be used as references, but this is not enough to prove union affiliation to a National Labor Relations Board agent. In fact, in some cases, organizers will advise applicants to write something on the application informing the employer of the applicant's union affiliation. Some salts choose to write the following on employment applications: "I am a volunteer union organizer. I intend to speak with the workers before work, during lunch, and after work to organize workers into a union". Save a copy as evidence.

Overt salts will wear a t-shirt with a union logo prominently displayed on it, but even this action may not convince an agent during testimony that the employer was aware the applicant was a union member. The reality is, the NLRB leans toward the side of big business, and there is no sign that this will change anytime soon. Our best bet is to do everything possible to solidify the applicant is indeed a full-fledged card-carrying union member bent on organizing the employer's company.

In the case of a covert salt, an applicant's union affiliation will be kept secret. This is a strategy you might choose to use to expose an employer you know to be cheating workers out of overtime for example.

I was approached by a member interested in salting, so I provided a contractor's address I was sure was underpaying his workers. Within days, I heard back that my salt was hired to work at the location in question. Because he was recently organized, he had used nonunion contractors on his application and decided on his own to apply covertly. Later we had a few meetings to take care of necessary paperwork and to form a strategy. He provided reports that I requested he fill out and names of all the workers, deliveries that were made, and the like. As early as the first paycheck, we had proof that the employer was shorting his pay. He continued to work on the project while we built a case. With photographs of the work being performed, we were finally able to receive back pay for some of the workers.

It was around this time that we sent a breakout letter – a certified, return receipt letter informing the contractor that our member was employed on the project and identifying him as a volunteer organizer for the union. You can imagine that things got interesting very fast. Unfortunately for us, our salt wasn't quite ready for the stress involved in being identified as a union agitator, and, within days, he quit. We did manage to get him to protest with us before his shift, however. I was disappointed we were not able to accomplish more, but he was a trooper.

362. Apply in Mass

Load up a van with union volunteers to apply at nonunion companies where applications are accepted. Show up unannounced. Be respectful and courteous. Make sure everyone brings their identification. Provide clipboards and pens.

363. Contact Former Employees

Former employees can offer valuable insights into the inner workings of a company. They often remain in contact with past coworkers providing a conduit for frank communication. Their assessments may provide useful information for future campaigns.

364. Expose Crooked Companies

In our effort to help workers, we come across crooked companies. They're easy to identify. Just keep track of the places candidates are leaving to join the union. At some point, a pattern will appear, and it will become obvious that so many individuals will have similar stories of being cheated, shorted on their checks, or not being paid at all. Most of the time, it's something small like a few hours stolen here or there. However, if the employer feels like it can get away with more they will.

There are some rotten employers out there. Even though they may represent a small percentage the damage caused is enormous. They cheat every chance they get, underpaying workers, substituting specified materials with cheap imitations, claiming fewer employees on their workers' comprehensive insurance policy. It seems they will do anything to save a buck. We are obligated as union organizers to expose these crooks so legitimate employers can compete on a level playing field.

Let's say an employer comes to your attention. Maybe you've heard accusations of questionable business practices from past employees. You want to confirm what you are hearing to make sure it's not just sour grapes on the part of a few disgruntled workers. Find out everything you can about the company, who the key decision makers are, and what specific allegations are being leveled. Are there documents or witnesses that can substantiate the claim? Other key information may be customers, employees list, news articles, hiring practices, suppliers, lawsuits, political contributions and community involvement. Keep an electronic copy as well as a printed version. Place all the research together in a tidy three-ring binder with a table of contents so anyone needing to reference the information will be able to do so with little effort. Gather this information and keep it handy so you have it whenever the need arises.

Share the research with others to help them make more educated decisions. It may help expose contractors who are not following the rules and level the playing field for those who are. If it prevents just one worker from being taken advantage of, we will be performing a valuable service to the industry.

365. Pray for Guidance

"Let us believe that God is in all our simple deeds and learn to find Him there."- Aiden Wilson Tozer

Tap into the power of faith. Whatever your beliefs are, integrate your goals into your spiritual practice. You will find encouragement for recruiting new members and organizing ideals in nearly every faith, whether it be performing good works or simply making a commitment to life-affirming action. Even if you're not religious at all, it's easy to find inspiration in the knowledge that your life's work will benefit your community and make the world a better place for future generations.

Faith allows you to step outside yourself, see a larger picture, and incorporate your organizing into your personal value system. Meditation, prayer, or quiet reflection on the ideals you cherish most can provide powerful support as you pursue your dreams, especially during times of adversity.

CPSIA information can be obtained
at www.ICGtesting.com
Printed in the USA
LVHW051615221020
669548LV00011B/1290